curriculum
connections

Atlas of World History

Industrialization and Empire
1783–1914

BROWN
BEAR
BOOKS

Published by Brown Bear Books Limited

An imprint of:
The Brown Reference Group Ltd
68 Topstone Road
Redding
Connecticut 06896
USA
www.brownreference.com

© 2009 The Brown Reference Group Ltd

ISBN: 978-1-933834-69-6

Editorial Director: Lindsey Lowe
Senior Managing Editor: Tim Cooke
Managing Editor: Rachel Tisdale
Editor: Louise Spilsbury
Designer: Rob Norridge

**Library of Congress Cataloging-in-Publication
Data available upon request**

Picture Credits

Cover Image
Mary Evans Picture Library

Artwork © The Brown Reference Group Ltd

The Brown Reference Group Ltd has made every effort to trace copyright holders of the pictures used in this book. Anyone having claims to ownership not identified above is invited to contact The Brown Reference Group Ltd.

Printed in the United States of America

Contents

Introduction

Atlas of World History forms part of the Curriculum Connections series. The six volumes of this set cover all the major periods of the World History curriculum: The First Civilizations (4,000,000–500 BCE); The Classical World (500 BCE–600 CE); The Middle Ages (600–1492); The Early Modern World (1492–1783); Industrialization and Empire (1783–1914); and World Wars and Globalization (1914–2010).

About this set

Each volume in *Atlas of World History* features thematic world and regional maps. All of the regional maps are followed by an in-depth article.

The volume opens with a series of maps that provide an overview of the world at particular dates. They show at-a-glance how the shape of the world changed during the period covered in the book. The rest of the volume is divided into regional sections, each of which covers a continent or part of a continent. Within each section, maps appear in broadly chronological order. Each map highlights a particular period or topic, which the accompanying article explains in a concise but accurate summary.

Within each article, two key aids to learning are located in sidebars in the margins of each page:

Curriculum Context sidebars indicate that a subject has particular relevance to certain key state and national World and American history guidelines and curricula. They highlight essential information or suggest useful ways for students to consider a subject or to include it in their studies.

Glossary sidebars define key words within the text.

At the end of the book, a summary Glossary lists the key terms defined in the volume. There is also a list of further print and Web-based resources and a full volume index.

About this book

Industrialization and Empire is a fascinating guide to the history of humankind from the time of the American Revolutionary War to the outbreak of World War I.

The volume begins with a series of maps that present an overview of the grand themes of history at key dates between 1783 and 1914. The maps chart the shifting pattern of human settlement and the rise and fall of empires and states, in addition to reviewing the spread of trade and exploration on a world scale.

The regional maps that follow look more closely at the great events of the period: the Napoleonic Wars and the rise of nationalism in Europe, the growth of British power in India, the European impact on Africa, and the wars of liberation and the Civil War in the Americas. There is also coverage of less familiar histories, such as those of colonial Southeast Asia, New Zealand, a nd Manchu China.

TYPOGRAPHICAL CONVENTIONS	
World maps	
FRANCE	state or empire
Belgian Congo	dependency or territory
Mongols	tribe, chiefdom or people
Anasazi culture	cultural group
Regional maps	
HUNGARY	state or empire
Bohemia	dependency or territory
Slavs	tribe, chiefdom or people
ANATOLIA	geographical region
✕	battle
•	site or town

The World in 1812

In 1812 European powers controlled much of the "New World," with the exception of the young United States. Although South Asia was fragmented, the Russian, Manchu, and Ottoman empires dominated much of the continent. In Europe, dynastic wars had established modern borders.

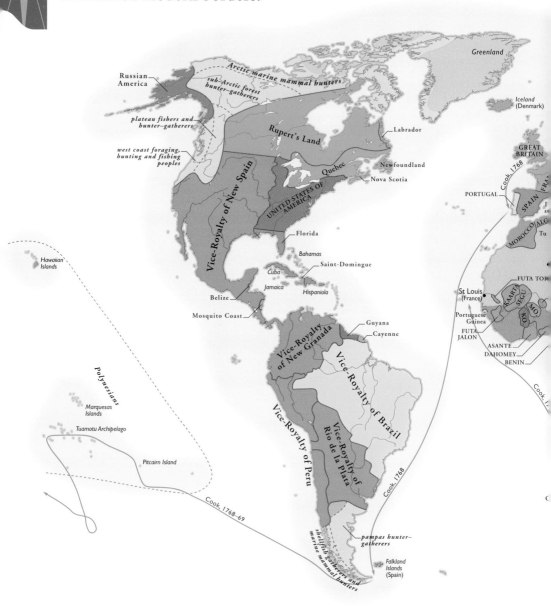

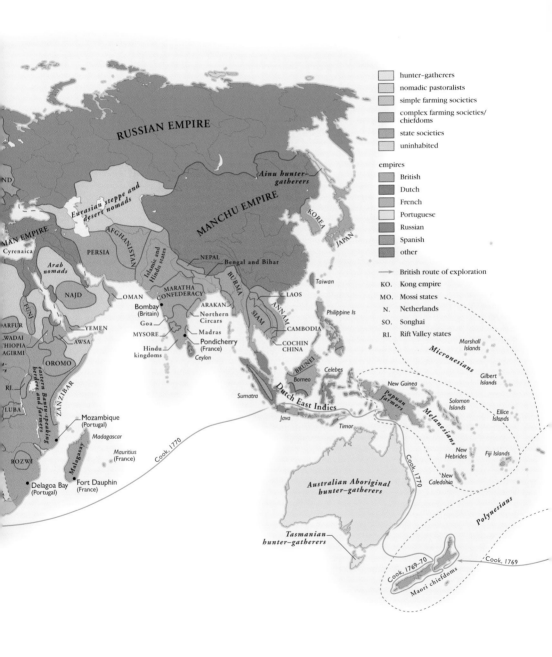

Legend

- hunter-gatherers
- nomadic pastoralists
- simple farming societies
- complex farming societies/ chiefdoms
- state societies
- uninhabited

empires

- British
- Dutch
- French
- Portuguese
- Russian
- Spanish
- other

→ British route of exploration

KO. Kong empire
MO. Mossi states
N.   Netherlands
SO. Songhai
RI. Rift Valley states

Map labels

RUSSIAN EMPIRE

Ainu hunter-gatherers

MANCHU EMPIRE

Eurasian steppe and desert nomads

ND

MAN EMPIRE
Cyrenaica

AFGHANISTAN

KOREA

JAPAN

Arab nomads

PERSIA

Islamic and Hindu states

NEPAL

Bengal and Bihar

BURMA

Taiwan

NAJD

OMAN

MARATHA CONFEDERACY

ARAKAN

LAOS

DARFUR

YEMEN

Bombay (Britain)

Northern Circars

SIAM

ANNAM

WADAI
THIOPIA
AGIRMI

AWSA

Goa

MYSORE

Madras

CAMBODIA

Philippine Is

OROMO

Pondicherry (France)

Hindu kingdoms

Ceylon

COCHIN CHINA

eastern Bantu-speaking herders and farmers

BRUNEI

Celebes

Borneo

Marshall Islands

RI.

LUBA

ZANZIBAR

New Guinea

Papuan farmers

Micronesians

Gilbert Islands

Mozambique (Portugal)

Sumatra

Dutch East Indies

Java

Timor

Solomon Islands

Melanesians

Ellice Islands

Madagascar

Malagasy

Mauritius (France)

Cook, 1770

Australian Aboriginal hunter-gatherers

Cook, 1770

New Hebrides

New Caledonia

Fiji Islands

ROZWI

Delagoa Bay (Portugal)

Fort Dauphin (France)

Polynesians

Tasmanian hunter-gatherers

Cook, 1769-70

Cook, 1769

Maori chiefdoms

The World in 1880

Toward the end of the 19th century, the British empire was truly global, spreading from Canada to India and Australasia, while European states made territorial inroads in Africa and elsewhere. The United States had reached its current size, while newly independent countries in Central and South America had thrown off Spanish and Portuguese rule.

N

Greenland
(Denmark)

Alaska

Iceland
(Denmark)

CANADA

Newfoundland

UNITED
KINGDOM

UNITED STATES

PORTUGAL

SPAIN

FRA

MOROCCO

Alge

Hawaiian Islands
(United States)

MEXICO

Bahamas

camel

British
Honduras

Cuba

HAITI

Puerto Rico

Senegal

FUTA TOR

Jamaica

GUATEMALA

COSTA RICA

DOMINICAN
REPUBLIC

Gambia

TUKULOR
CALIPHATE

EL SALVADOR
HONDURAS
NICARAGUA

VENEZUELA

British Guiana
Dutch Guiana
French Guiana

PG.
FU.

SAMORI
EMPIRE

Sierra
Leone

AS.

COLOMBIA

LIBERIA

BE.

Galapagos
Islands
(Ecuador)

ECUADOR

Ivory Coast
Gold Coast

Marquesas Islands
(France)

BRAZIL

MB

PERU

Tuamotu Archipelago
(France)

BOLIVIA

PARAGUAY

Ovi
ki

CHILE

ARGENTINA

PARAGUAY

URUGUAY

ORA

shellfish gatherers and
marine mammal hunters

pampas hunter–
gatherers

Falkland
Islands
(Britain)

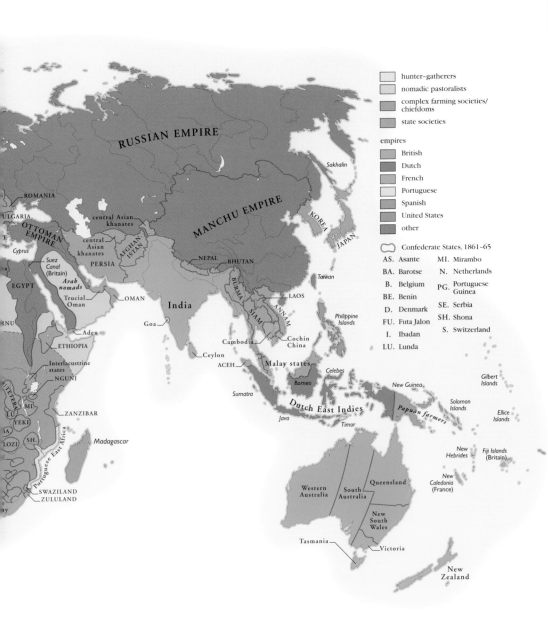

hunter-gatherers

nomadic pastoralists

complex farming societies/
chiefdoms

state societies

empires

British

Dutch

French

Portuguese

Spanish

United States

other

Confederate States, 1861–65

AS.	Asante	MI.	Mirambo
BA.	Barotse	N.	Netherlands
B.	Belgium	PG.	Portuguese Guinea
BE.	Benin		
D.	Denmark	SE.	Serbia
FU.	Futa Jalon	SH.	Shona
I.	Ibadan	S.	Switzerland
LU.	Lunda		

RUSSIAN EMPIRE

ROMANIA

ULGARIA

OTTOMAN
EMPIRE

Cyprus

Suez
Canal
(Britain)

EGYPT

Arab
nomads

Trucial
Oman

OMAN

Aden

ETHIOPIA

Interlacustrine
states

NGUNI

RNU

LU

YEKE

ZANZIBAR

Portuguese East Africa

BA

LOZI

SH.

ay

Madagascar

SWAZILAND

ZULULAND

central Asian
khanates

central
Asian
khanates

AFGHANISTAN

PERSIA

India

Goa

Ceylon

central Asian khanates

MANCHU EMPIRE

KOREA

JAPAN

Sakhalin

Taiwan

NEPAL

BHUTAN

BURMA

SIAM

LAOS

ANNAM

Cochin
China

Cambodia

ACEH

Malay states

Sumatra

Java

Dutch East Indies

Timor

Borneo

Celebes

Philippine
Islands

New Guinea

Papuan farmers

Solomon
Islands

Gilbert
Islands

Ellice
Islands

New
Hebrides

New
Caledonia
(France)

Fiji Islands
(Britain)

Western
Australia

South
Australia

Queensland

New
South
Wales

Tasmania

Victoria

New
Zealand

The World in 1914

The world map of 1914, at the outset of World War I, reveals similar country boundaries to those of today. The British, French, and Dutch empires reached their greatest size, just as Germany set its sights on armed expansion. In only a few decades, European powers had claimed much of Africa.

RUSSIAN EMPIRE

ROMANIA

BULGARIA

OTTOMAN
EMPIRE

ania

Egypt

Kuwait

Qatar

PERSIA

AFGHAN-
ISTAN

MONGOLIA

CHINESE REPUBLIC

Sakhalin

Korea
(Japan)

JAPAN

TIBET

NEPAL

BHUTAN

Taiwan
(Japan)

Arab
nomads

Trucial
Oman

Oman

Goa

India

Burma

Hong Kong
(Britain)

Eritrea

Aden

SIAM

Philippine
Islands

Sudan

British Somaliland

French
Indo-China

Mariana Islands
(Germany)

ETHIOPIA

French Somaliland

Ceylon

Malay states

Guam
(United States)

Marshall
Islands
(Germany)

ganda

gian
ngo

Italian Somaliland

Celebes

Borneo

Palau
(Germany)

Gilbert
Islands
(Britain)

ern
sia

German
East
Africa

British East Africa

Sumatra

New Guinea

German New
Guinea

Solomon
Islands
(Britain)

Ellice
Islands
(Britain)

Nyasaland

Madagascar

Java

Dutch East Indies

Timor

Papua

n of
h Africa

Mozambique

Swaziland

Basutoland

AUSTRALIA

New Hebrides
(Britain/France)

New
Caledonia
(France)

Fiji Islands
(Britain)

Tasmania

NEW
ZEALAND

nomadic pastoralists

state societies

empires

Belgian

British

Dutch

French

German

Italian

Portuguese

Spanish

United States

other

A.   Albania   N.   Netherlands
B.   Belgium   SE. Serbia
D.   Denmark   S.   Switzerland
M.   Montenegro

World Population

The peak of modern migration came at the start of the 20th century, when millions of people from the world's ever-increasing population moved to new countries.

Greenland

CANADA

Newfoundland

Ireland

UNITED STATES

from Japan

from China

MEXICO

Hawaiian
Islands

CUBA   Bahamas

HAITI
Puerto Rico
Jamaica
DOMINICAN
REPUBLIC

MOROCCO

Rio de
Oro

British Guiana
Dutch Guiana
French Guiana

BRAZIL

PERU

URUGUAY

CHILE

ARGENTINA

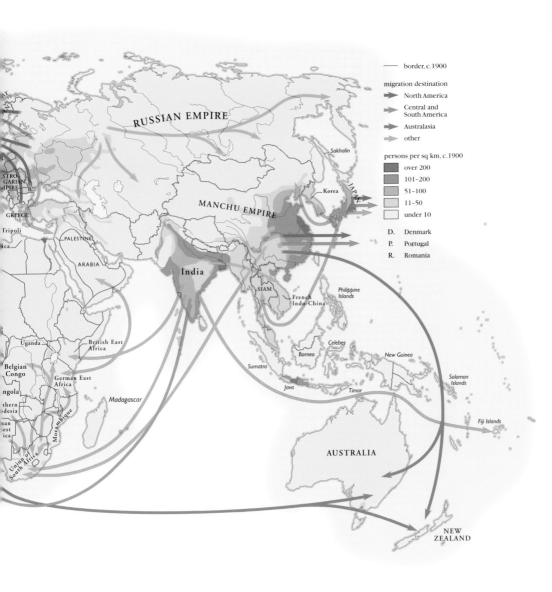

border, c.1900

migration destination
North America
Central and
South America
Australasia
other

persons per sq km, c.1900
over 200
101–200
51–100
11–50
under 10

D.   Denmark
P.   Portugal
R.   Romania

RUSSIAN EMPIRE

MANCHU EMPIRE

AUSTRO-
HUNGARIAN
EMPIRE

GREECE

Tripoli

PALESTINE

ARABIA

India

SIAM

French
Indo-China

Philippine
Islands

Celebes

Borneo

Sumatra

Java

Timor

New Guinea

Solomon
Islands

Fiji Islands

AUSTRALIA

NEW
ZEALAND

Sakhalin

Korea

JAPAN

Uganda

British East
Africa

Belgian
Congo

ngola

German East
Africa

Madagascar

Mozambique

thern
desia

an
est
ica

Union of
South Africa

World Population

The world's population grew from around 950 million in 1830 to around 1,600 million in 1914. The increase was the result of many factors: improved food production and diet; a greater awareness of hygiene and the start of public health programs; and new labor opportunities in industrialized regions that allowed people to escape rural hardship.

Curriculum Context

Many curricula include discussion of the diverse and complex political and social reasons why Europeans emigrated in the 19th century.

Yet in spite of these improvements, millions still lived in abject poverty; the biggest migrations ever recorded began in the 19th century. Europe experienced increased cycles of emigration after each economic depression, as emigrants tried to escape poverty, unemployment, and poor housing. Many fled from Russia and Ireland to escape persecution or starvation. In all, over 40 million people left Europe between 1830 and 1914, yet during the same period the population of the continent increased by some 76 percent.

Emigration to the Americas

Migrants looked above all to the Americas as lands of opportunities. Up to 1895, immigrants to the United States and Canada tended to come from Scandinavia, Germany, Britain, and Ireland. Among those who endured the greatest hardship were the Irish, a trend dramatized by the Irish famine in 1845–47. Many prospective immigrants suffered from cholera and typhoid, and did not survive the passage. After 1895 most immigrants were of central and southern European origin. As a result of the huge influx (especially between 1900 and 1914), some regions of the United States were chiefly composed of either first- or second-generation European immigrants by 1914.

Irish famine

The failure of the staple potato crop in Ireland, owing to a plant disease; one third of the population starved to death.

Empire opportunities

European imperial acquisitions also attracted their own immigration, with Italians moving to Libya and French settlers to north Africa. The territories gained by Germany in inhospitable equatorial zones proved less inviting to emigrants from the home country. Many British people, especially Scots and Welsh, emigrated to Canada, South Africa, Australia, and New Zealand in order to find work.

Migrants from Asia

The Chinese emigrated in great numbers in this period; as early as 1850 Australian employers began shipping in Chinese "coolies" to undertake the hard labor formerly done by convicts. Laws were soon passed, however, to prevent further Chinese immigration. In the United States, the Chinese were brought in to mine the California goldfields and build the transcontinental railroads. Later waves of Chinese migrants joined Indians in seeking jobs, often as indentured laborers, on the plantations of Cuba, Siam, British Guiana, and French Indo-China. Others worked alongside African migrants in South African gold mines. Overpopulation in Japan led to large-scale emigration in the 1880s, first to Hawaii and then to California. However, after the host country threatened total exclusion, Japanese emigrants went instead to Manchuria, Brazil, and Peru.

Curriculum Context

The discovery of gold in South Africa had an impact on political and race relations among British colonial authorities, Afrikaners, and Africans.

Changes in Russia and Europe

Russian Jews started to emigrate after the pogroms began in the 1880s. Over two million fled to the United States, while some 60,000 joined the new Zionist movement to establish a Jewish homeland in Palestine. In Russia, millions of non-Jews sought a new life in undeveloped regions. Three million emigrated to North America, while many European workers settled in Russia: Germans and Austrians came to found new "colonist villages" or to work in newly established industrial towns. Europe was now accustomed to workers, capital, and expertise constantly crossing national frontiers, a situation that would end abruptly with the outbreak of war in 1914.

Pogrom

Organized attack on or massacre of a community of people, usually for religious or ethnic reasons.

World Trade

Industrialization and developments in transportation caused a huge increase in the volume and variety of world trade, establishing global links between nations.

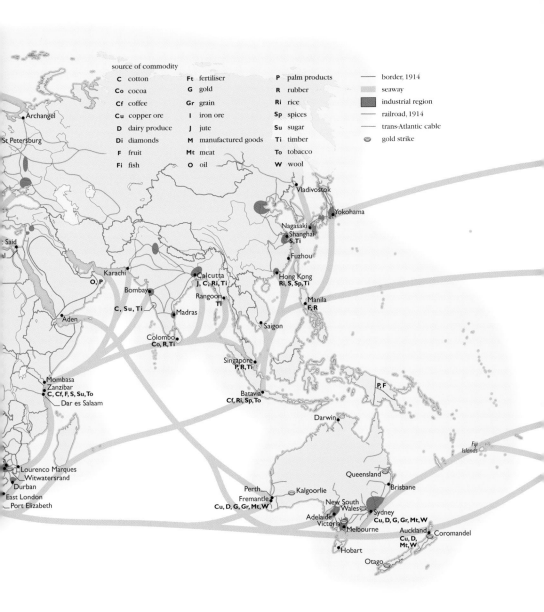

source of commodity

C	cotton	**Ft**	fertiliser	**P**	palm products
Co	cocoa	**G**	gold	**R**	rubber
Cf	coffee	**Gr**	grain	**Ri**	rice
Cu	copper ore	**I**	iron ore	**Sp**	spices
D	dairy produce	**J**	jute	**Su**	sugar
Di	diamonds	**M**	manufactured goods	**Ti**	timber
F	fruit	**Mt**	meat	**To**	tobacco
Fi	fish	**O**	oil	**W**	wool

— border, 1914
  seaway
  industrial region
— railroad, 1914
— trans-Atlantic cable
  gold strike

Archangel

St Petersburg

Said

Vladivostok

Yokohama

Nagasaki
Shanghai
S, Ti

Fuzhou

Karachi
O, P

Bombay

Calcutta
J, C, Ri, Ti

Hong Kong
Ri, S, Sp, Ti

Rangoon
Ti

Manila
F, R

C, Su, Ti

Madras

Saigon

Aden

Colombo
Co, R, Ti

Singapore
P, R, Ti

Mombasa
Zanzibar
C, Cf, F, S, Su, To
Dar es Salaam

Batavia
Cf, Ri, Sp, To

P, F

Darwin

Fiji
Islands

Lourenco Marques
Witwatersrand
Durban
East London
Port Elizabeth

Queensland

Brisbane

Perth
Fremantle
Cu, D, G, Gr, Mt, W

Kalgoorlie

New South
Wales

Sydney
Cu, D, G, Gr, Mt, W

Adelaide
Victoria

Melbourne

Auckland
**Cu, D,
Mt, W**

Coromandel

Hobart

Otago

World Trade

Between 1830 and 1914 world trade was dominated by the industrialized nations of Europe and the United States. These countries traded manufactured goods and foodstuffs with each other and, increasingly, with the developing native and colonial societies of Latin America, Asia, and Africa.

The growth in production in the industrialized nations was accompanied by a rise in foreign trade, which rose from 10 percent of all earnings in 1830 to 33 percent in 1914. This was based in large part on the systematic exploitation of traditional societies and their raw materials; the trade passing through the major ports constructed in China, Latin America, and Africa hardly benefited the economies of the host countries.

Imperialism and exploitation

As a result, rural economies were often destroyed—as in Africa, India, and the Dutch East Indies—and replaced by westernized agricultural patterns that dictated the nature of the crops grown and the manner in which they were marketed. Accompanied by colonial warfare, this exploitation was the ultimate expression of imperialism between 1830 and 1914.

Improving infrastructures

The infrastructure of global trade was financed by the industrialized nations. For example, the economic development of Africa required European-built railroads to carry exports to the coast. Similarly, investment by the industrialized nations built harbors, provided ships, and established coaling stations worldwide. To handle the new commerce, port facilities were also transformed in the industrialized countries. Existing harbors, such as that in New York, were enlarged, while new ports were built at Trieste in Italy and Le Havre in France.

Changing the face of shipping

Ship design also underwent radical change, with the advent of steam propulsion in 1833, iron hulls in 1837, and steel hulls in 1856. By mid-century, steamships were providing stiff competition for the Clipper sailing vessels. Sail was dealt a further blow when new canals at Suez, Kiel, and Panama spared the need for long voyages around the continents. The world's merchant fleet expanded from 9 million net tonnes in 1850 to over 35 million tonnes in 1914.

Global food supplies

Rapid sea communications, coupled with the effects of migration and the opening up of fertile lands in Canada, the United States, Russia, Australia, the Danube lands, and Argentina, meant that cheap food became available to industrialized countries. A major effect of global trade from the 1870s was to reduce drastically the price of wheat and other staple foods.

The spread of technology

Another important result of global trade was the growth in the sales of modern technology to traditional societies. This was often in the form of transport technology, such as railroads, or factory machinery, but also came to comprise advanced military hardware. The balance of power in regional conflicts was radically altered by this development.

Clipper

Type of very fast sailing ship that had multiple masts and a square rig; clippers were used for carrying perishable cargoes such as tea.

Curriculum Context

It may be helpful to understand the way in which the development of industrialization helped to expand the world market economy.

The gold standard

Increased global trade required changes in the way the world economy was run. The world's most heavily traded currencies were now based on the gold standard, a system in which bank notes or deposits are convertible into gold at a central bank. The major gold strikes in California, Australia, South Africa, and Canada increased the money supply and so sustained the growth in commercial activity. Adequate gold reserves guaranteed that a country could trade without running into debt. Monetary unions, with currencies based on the gold standard, also became popular.

The Age of Revolution

During the last years of the 18th century a series of revolutions and rebellions changed the political face of Europe, particularly in France.

ATLANTIC
OCEAN

Scotland

Edinburgh
Glasgow

Belfast
Carrick
×1798
Newcastle
Killala
Bay
Ireland
Dublin
GREAT BRITAIN
& IRELAND
Manchester
Liverpool

Wexford
1798
Birmingham

Wales
Fishguard
England
Bristol

The Nore
1797
178

Ilfracombe
Spithead
1797
London

Hondschoote
1793
Jemappes
1792
Wattignies
1793
Paris
×1789
Versailles
1789

"First of June"
1794

Brest

Quiberon Bay
1795

Orléans

FRANC

Nantes
Vendée

Bordeaux

SA
PIE

Venaissin
to Papal States
Avig
M

Toulouse

La Coruña

Troul
1793
Verne
1793

ANDORRA

Oporto

Barcelona

PORTUGAL

Madrid

SPAIN
Valencia

M

Lisbon
Guadiana

Baleari
Islands

Cape St Vincent
1797
Cádiz

Gibraltar
to Britain

Algiers

Tangier
Ceuta
to Spain
Melilla
to Spain
Oran

A

MOROCCO

Legend

═══	borders, 1783
⌑	border of Holy Roman empire, 1783
▢	Austrian Habsburg territory, 1783
▢	France, 1783
▢	Brandenburg-Prussia, 1783
▢	Great Britain & Hanover, 1783
▢	Ottoman empire, 1783
▢	Spanish Bourbon territory, 1783
▢	Russian empire, 1783
⌒	Russian gains by 1795
⌒	Brandenburg-Prussian gains by 1795
⌒	Austrian Habsburg gains by 1797
⌒	French gains by 1800
Roman Republic	state established by Revolutionary France
▦	extent of the "Great Fear" within France, 1789
▨	French counter-revolution, 1793
➜	French campaign, 1796–98
➜	Russian campaign, 1798–1800
⚲	town bombarded by Russian Black Sea fleet
⚑	Naval mutiny in Great Britain
✳	major revolt, riot or disorder

Christiania

SWEDEN

Stockholm

Vänern

Vättern

Göteborg

DENMARK-NORWAY

Copenhagen

Helsinki

Svenskund
1789, 1790

St Petersburg

Revel

RUSSIAN
EMPIRE

Lake
Peipus

Riga

Gotland
to Sweden

Baltic Sea

Western Dvina

Samogitia

Hamburg
Bremen

Hanover

1784

Brandenburg

Berlin

Neerwinden
1793

Frankfurt
Nuremberg

Wissembourg
1793

Swedish
Pomerania

Pomerania

West
Prussia

Danzig

Stettin

Netze

Oder

New East Prussia
from 1795

Königsberg

East
Prussia

Ermland

West
Prussia

PRUSSIA

Elbe

Mazovia

Minsk

Lithuania

Black
Russia

Warsaw

POLAND

1794

Podlesia

Volhynia

Great Poland
South Prussia from 1793

Little Poland
West Galicia from 1795

Vistula

Red Russia

Silesia

Saxony

Dresden

Munich

Bavaria

Hohenlinden
1800

Zürich
1799

Prague

Bohemia

Austrian
Silesia

Moravia

Galicia and Lodomeria

Austria

Danube

Vienna

Salzburg

Buda

HABSBURG EMPIRE

Bukovina

Jassy

Bessarabia

Sebastopol

Russian Black Sea fleet, 1798–1800

Black Sea

SWISS
FEDERATION
1803 Helvetic Republic

Tyrol

Leoben

Styria

Hungary

1790

Moldavia

Castiglione
1796

Rivoli
1797

Campo Formio

Carinthia

Carniola

Transylvania

Mantua

Arcole
1796

Venice
1797–1802

Cisalpine Republic

Slavonia

Banat

Wallachia

Danube

Varna

Milan

VENICE

Croatia

Sava

GENOA
1797–1805
Ligurian Republic

Genoa

Bosnia

Serbia

Bulgaria

Fano

TUSCANY

PAPAL
STATES

1798–99
Roman
Republic

Herzegovina

RAGUSA

MONTENEGRO

Russian Black Sea fleet, 1798–1800

1798

Corsica
Britain
Ajaccio

Civitavecchia

Naples

1798–99 Parthenopean Republic

Rome

Albania

Üsküb

Edirne

Constantinople

ANATOLIA

1798

1793

Sardinia

1793

Naples

KINGDOM OF
NAPLES AND
SICILY

Janina

Rumelia

OTTOMAN EMPIRE

Tunis

Palermo

Messina

Sicily,
1799 independent
of Naples

Ionian Islands
Venetian,
1797 to France,
1799 to Russia

Morea

Athens

Rhodes

Cyprus

Sy

Tunis

Bonaparte, 1798

Cythera
Venetian,
1797 to France,
1799 to Russia

Crete

Mediterranean Sea

Malta
Knights of St John,
1798 to France,
1800 to Britain

Acre
Mount Tabor
1798

Jaffa

Palestine

Tripoli

Cyrene

Aboukir Bay
(Battle of the Nile)
1798

Alexandria

Bonaparte, 1798

Battle of the
Pyramids
1798

Cairo

Nile

Egypt

The Age of Revolution

Enlightenment thinkers of the mid-18th century often emphasized people's right to self-determination through a system of representative government. In this they expressed a hostility to the traditional forces—clerics, aristocrats, and absolute monarchs—that still reigned supreme throughout Europe in the 18th century.

Fueled by poverty, inflation, and food shortages, and inspired by the successful revolution of American colonists against the British (1775–1783), this discontent was soon to erupt.

Failed insurrections

Uprisings occurred in 1784, when the Patriot party in the Dutch Netherlands tried to democratize government, and in 1787, when citizens of the neighboring territory of the Austrian Netherlands (Belgium) attempted to establish an independent republic. Neither insurrection achieved its goals.

Storming the Bastille

A more widely based protest began against the *ancien régime* (autocratic royal government) in France when Louis XVI tried to raise taxes to avert state bankruptcy. He summoned the Estates-General—a periodic assembly of deputies from the three "Estates" (clergy, nobility, and commoners)—to approve his plans. However, Louis was faced with a political crisis when the Third Estate (in reality made up of members of the bourgeoisie, or rising middle classes, instead of true commoners) withdrew to found a National Assembly and institute reform. Parisians feared an attack on the Assembly by Louis XVI's forces and so, on July 14, 1789, they attacked and captured the Bastille fortress in eastern Paris, in part to obtain weapons stored within its walls. The rebellion spread rapidly.

The Rights of Man

In August 1789 the Assembly abolished the feudal system and issued its Declaration of the Rights of Man, which proclaimed freedom of conscience, property, and speech, and established the principle that sovereign power resided in the nation rather than the king. After failing to escape from the country in 1791, Louis was compelled to approve a constitution that divested him of most of his power.

Curriculum Context

Students may find it useful to compare the values of the Declaration of the Rights of Man with those expressed in the American Declaration of Independence and the Bill of Rights.

During the French Revolution, the *sans-culotte,* or "man without breeches," became a symbol of radical republicans. More wealthy Frenchmen wore knee-length breeches rather than trousers.

Revolutionary wars

By this stage, aristocrats who had managed to flee France had persuaded Prussia and the Habsburg empire (Austria) to intervene on Louis' behalf. Opposition to revolutionary France soon crystallized into the First Coalition of European powers. The ensuing Revolutionary Wars (1792–1802) saw the French repulse an initial invasion and then go on the attack. The king and queen and many of their aristocratic supporters were executed, counter-revolutionary risings were suppressed, internecine struggles broke out among the revolutionaries (the "Terror"), and the French tried to export revolution to their hostile neighbors in the Netherlands, Spain, and Britain (where they fomented rebellion in Ireland).

The Second Coalition

The First Coalition was broken by a series of French victories in 1794–95, culminating in a successful invasion of the Netherlands (ruled by France as the Batavian Republic until 1806). Prussia and Spain sued for peace, leaving Britain and the Habsburg empire isolated. Britain, though, maintained naval supremacy with victories over France, and latterly its Dutch and Spanish allies, from 1794–97. In 1798 a Second Coalition was formed.

The rise of Napoleon

Napoleon Bonaparte now began to emerge as the greatest of the French commanders through his brilliant campaigns in Italy and Austria. By late 1797, he had forced Austria to cede the Austrian Netherlands to France in exchange for Venice in a peace treaty that also created French satellite states in northern Italy. As a prelude to his planned invasion of Britain, Bonaparte threatened Britain's trade route to India by attacking Egypt in 1798. Though victorious against Egypt's Mamluke rulers, his fleet was defeated by the British admiral Nelson at the Battle of the Nile. In response to reverses in Italy and on the Rhine, Bonaparte returned to France, overthrew the committee that had ruled France since 1795 (the "Directory"), and installed himself as military dictator.

Conquests and defeats

French military fortunes proceeded to rise; Napoleon's generals blocked an Anglo-Russian expedition to the Batavian Republic and defeated the Russians at Zürich, while he himself masterminded the defeat of the Austrians at Marengo (1800). Yet though his forces were all-powerful on land, his lack of naval superiority meant that he could not prevent raids from the Russian Black Sea fleet in 1798–1800, or—more importantly—deliver a decisive blow against the Second Coalition.

European enlightenment

In eastern Europe, Poland embarked on a course of constitutional reform in the 1790s modeled on Enlightenment ideas. Russia under Catherine II, which had annexed part of Poland in 1772, responded by invading in 1792. Further regions were annexed by Russia and Prussia in the Second Partition (1793). A rebellion against the foreign overlords ended with the capitulation of Warsaw in 1794, and the Third Partition (1795) saw the disappearance of Poland as a sovereign country for over 120 years.

Curriculum Context

Napoleon's influence fundamentally changed the aims and outcomes of the revolution. It is important to realize that the revolution constantly changed.

Enlightenment

Movement that rejected traditional ideas and values in favor of reason and individualism and brought about many humanitarian reforms.

Napoleonic Europe

Through a series of
campaigns between 1803
and 1815, Napoleon
Bonaparte spread French
influence across much
of Europe.

borders, 1812

French empire, 1812

state dependent on France, 1812

French ally, 1812

Ottoman empire, 1812

Russian empire, 1812

United Kingdom of Great Britain
and Ireland, 1812

Confederation of the Rhine

France, 1815

Spanish guerrilla activity

French victory

French defeat

Austrian campaign

British campaign

French campaign

Napoleon's escape from Elba,
and the Waterloo campaign, 1815

Prussian campaign

Russian campaign

Volga

Christiania

SWEDEN
1815 union with Norway

DENMARK–NORWAY
allied to France until 1814

Göteborg

Vänern

Vättern

Stockholm

Gotland

Helsinki

Revel

St Petersburg

Lake Peipus

Baltic Sea

Riga

Western Dvina

Vitebsk
Smolensk
1812

Borodino
1812

Moscow
1812

Maloyaroslavets
1812

Copenhagen
1801, 1807

1807–11

Tilsit
Kovno
Königsberg
Danzig
Friedland
1807
Eylau
1807

Vilna
1812

1812

Krasnoi
1812

1812

MECKLENBURG-
SCHWERIN

Swedish Pomerania
1815 to Prussia

Berezina
1812

Minsk

Hamburg
Bremen

Pomerania
PRUSSIA
1807–13 allied
to France

East
Prussia

RUSSIAN
EMPIRE

WESTPHALIA

Brandenburg
Berlin

GRAND DUCHY
OF WARSAW
1815 to Russia

Warsaw

Kiev

Kharkov

HESSE

Oder

Jena-Auerstädt
1806

Lützen
1813

SAXONY
Leipzig
1813
Dresden
1813

Bautzen
1813

Silesia

Weichsel

Dnieper

Galicia and Lodomeria

Hanau
1813

WÜRZBURG

Prague

Austrian
Silesia

Moravia

Dniester

Ebersberg
1809

Ratisbon
1809
Ulm
1805

Munich

BAVARIA

Bohemia

Austerlitz
1805

Wagram
1809

Bessarabia
1812 to Russian empire

Ochakov

Mannheim

Salzburg

Danube

Vienna
Aspern
1809

AUSTRIAN EMPIRE
1809–13 allied to France

Bukovina

Jassy

HELVETIA

Styria

Buda

Hungary

Moldavia

Sebastopol

Carinthia

Transylvania

1811

Milan

Venice

Illyrian Provinces

Slavonia

Banat

Belgrade

1806–12 under
Russian occupation

Bucharest

Wallachia

1811

Varna

Russian maritime operations 1800–07

Black
Sea

enoa

ITALY

LUCCA

Florence

Sava

Save

Danube

Serbia

1811

Bulgaria

Tuscany

Herzegovina

Bosnia

PIOMBINO
Papal
States

Elba

Rome

NAPLES

MONTENEGRO

Üsküb

Rumelia

Edirne

Constantinople

ANATOLIA

sica

cio

Naples

BENEVENTO

Albania

Janina

OTTOMAN
EMPIRE

inia

Corfu
to Russia,
1807 to France,
1815 to Britain

Palermo
Messina

SICILY

Ionian Islands
to Russia,
1807 to France,
1809 to Britain

Morea

Athens

Rhodes

Tunis

1800–07

Cythera
to Russia,
1807 to France,
1809 to Britain

Crete

Malta
to Britain

*Mediterranean
Sea*

Tunis

Cyrene

Cyrenaica

Aboukir
1799, 1801
Alexandria

EGYPT

Napoleonic Europe

French victories in 1800 virtually secured the defeat of Austria, but British naval power still frustrated Bonaparte. His army was forced out of Egypt by the British in 1801, while in the same year the Danish fleet he hoped would keep Britain from the Baltic was destroyed at Copenhagen.

A respite from war was confirmed by the Treaty of Amiens in 1802, enabling Britain to implement the Act of Union which incorporated Ireland into the United Kingdom, improving the islands' security.

The beginnings of an empire

Napoleon revived his plan to invade Britain, which now stood alone against France, but Britain's comprehensive naval victory at Trafalgar (1805) and the formation of the Third Coalition later that year focused Napoleon's attention back on the armies of Austria, which he overwhelmed at Ulm and Austerlitz. In 1806, Napoleon proclaimed the dissolution of the Holy Roman empire, united all the German states (apart from Austria and Prussia) into the Confederation of the Rhine, and moved north to smash the Prussians at Jena–Auerstädt. After Napoleon's defeat of a Russian army at Friedland in 1807, the Treaty of Tilsit broke the Third Coalition.

Curriculum Context

The Napoleonic wars were important for their impact on concepts of nationalism, constitutionalism, and religious institutions in Europe.

The Continental System

In 1806–7 Napoleon was at the height of his power. He now turned to blockading all trade with Britain. The so-called Continental System, established in Napoleon's Berlin and Milan decrees (1806, 1807) was a major embargo on Britain's trade with the European nations under Napoleon's control, which he hoped would weaken Britain. It was designed to force the British to buy overpriced smuggled goods, thus depleting their gold reserves. Britain retaliated by banning French trade between one port and another.

The Code Napoléon

Between 1804 (when he declared himself emperor) and 1814, Napoleon imposed his administrative and political ideas upon a conquered Europe. In all his vassal states, he introduced the Code Napoléon, which enshrined the principles of equality and liberty in law and provided protection for private property.

A new phase

In 1808, a French army forced Portugal to adopt the Continental System. This sparked an uprising in Spain, while the British established a base in Portugal. Victory against the Austrians allowed Napoleon to concentrate his forces on Spain and temporarily reverse his setbacks suffered there, but his decision to attack Russia in 1812—again to enforce the Continental System—radically altered the situation. After hunger, winter, and Russian resistance forced a withdrawal from Moscow in late 1812, Napoleon's enemies seized the opportunity to create a Fourth Coalition.

Defeat and exile

In 1813, Napoleon's forces resisted the new coalition at Lützen, Bautzen, and Dresden but suffered heavy casualties. However, in the "Battle of the Nations" at Leipzig Napoleon suffered his first major defeat and was forced to quit Germany. At the same time, the British pushed north to Toulouse and concluded the Peninsular War. Allied armies pressed home their attack from Germany, and threatened Paris in 1814. Napoleon abdicated and was sent into exile on the Mediterranean island of Elba. While the victorious allies were redrawing the map of Europe at the Congress of Vienna, Napoleon escaped from exile. In his so-called Hundred Days, he reformed his armies but lost at the Battle of Waterloo against the combined British, Dutch, and Prussian forces in 1815. He was exiled to St. Helena in the south Atlantic, where he died. Europe was finally at peace after 23 years of war.

Congress of Vienna

International conference from September 1814 to June 1815 to shape Europe after the downfall of Napoleon I.

Nationalism in Europe

During the first half of the 19th century people across Europe struggled to establish their own national identities independent from imperial rule.

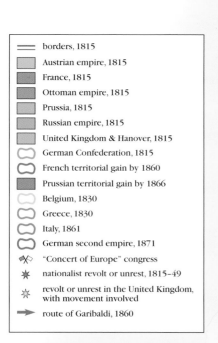

borders, 1815

Austrian empire, 1815

France, 1815

Ottoman empire, 1815

Prussia, 1815

Russian empire, 1815

United Kingdom & Hanover, 1815

German Confederation, 1815

French territorial gain by 1860

Prussian territorial gain by 1866

Belgium, 1830

Greece, 1830

Italy, 1861

German second empire, 1871

"Concert of Europe" congress

nationalist revolt or unrest, 1815–49

revolt or unrest in the United Kingdom, with movement involved

route of Garibaldi, 1860

NORWAY

Union from 1815

Christiania

SWEDEN

Vänern

Stockholm

Vättern

Göteborg

Gotland

Helsinki

St Petersburg
1825

Revel

Riga

Lake
Peipus

Vo

Baltic Sea

DENMARK

Copenhagen

chleswig
5 to Prussia

ein
tria,
ssia

Hamburg

Bremen

urg
1866 to Prussia

Königsberg

MECKLENBURG-
SCHWERIN

Danzig

East Prussia

Pomerania

Stettin

HANOVER
1866 to Prussia

PRUSSIA

Brandenburg

Poznan
1848

1830

1830

BRUNSWICK

Berlin
1848

Vistula

Warsaw
1830-31, 1848

Westphalia

1830

Elbe

Dresden
1848

Poland

ix-la-Chapelle
318

1830

SAXONY

Silesia

Oder

1847 to Austrian empire

Lvov
(Lemberg)
1848

Frankfurt
1833, 1848

HESSE

Prague
1848

Moravia

Krakow
1846, 1848

Galicia and Lodomeria

RUSSIAN
EMPIRE

1849

BAVARIA

BADEN

WÜRTTEMBERG

Hohenzollern

Bohemia

Brünn
(Brno)
1848

Troppau
1820

Dniester

Zürich

Berne

Munich
1848

Linz
1848

Salzburg

Austria
1848

Vienna
1848

Pressburg
1848

AUSTRIAN EMPIRE

Bukovina

Jassy
1848

Ochakov

SWITZERLAND

Milan
1848

Tyrol

Salzburg

Styria

Debrecen
1848

Buda
1848

Koloszvar
1848

Transylvania

MOLDAVIA
1829
autonomous

Sebastopol

Brescia
1815-30

Carinthia

Carniola

Laibach
1821

Agram
1848

Hungary

Temesvár
1849

Blaj
1848

Magenta
1859

Venetia
1815-30

Verona
1822

Solferino
1859

Venice
1848

Slavonia

WALLACHIA
1829 autonomous

Bucharest
1848

Black
Sea

Turin
1815-30

Lombardy

Croatia

Save

Belgrade

Varna

Genoa
1834

Parma

MODENA

1831

Dalmatia

Bosnia

SERBIA
1817 autonomous

Danube

Bulgaria

LUCCA

Florence
1849

Tuscany

Macerata
1831

Herzegovina

MONTENEGRO

Corsica

1870 to Italy

Rome
1848

Volturno
1860

Bari
1815-30

Üsküb

OTTOMAN
EMPIRE

Talamone

PAPAL STATES

Macedonia

SARDINIA

Naples
1820, 1848

Salerno
1815-30

BENEVENTO

Albania

Janina

Ionian Islands
1815-63 to Britain
1863 to Greece

ardinia

Palermo
1848-49

KINGDOM OF THE TWO SICILIES

Missolonghi
1826

Athens

Catalfimi
1860

Reggio
1815-30

Sicily

Milazzo
1860

Morea

Tunis

Navarino
1827

Cythera
1815-63 to Britain
1863 to Greece

Tunis

Malta
to Britain

Mediterranean
Sea

0
48

Nationalism in Europe

The decades after 1815 saw the emergence of nationalism in the aftermath of Napoleon's imperial rule. Liberals and democrats sought to create nation–states embracing a common racial and linguistic identity and embodying constitutionally guaranteed rights for their citizens.

Only a few nation–states were created in the early 19th century: Belgium, the Netherlands, Switzerland, and Greece. More often, the monarchies restored after the fall of Napoleon (Prussia, Austria, and Russia) stifled the nascent democracies. The strongest states to emerge—Italy and the German second empire—did so by coalescing around dynamic existing monarchies (Sardinia–Piedmont, and Prussia respectively).

Creating a balance of power

The Congress of Vienna (1814–15) set out to create a balance of power. It restored hereditary monarchies, created new kingdoms by unifying Norway with Sweden and Belgium with Holland, and established the "concert of Europe": congresses to deal with threats to political stability. For example, when revolutions broke out in Naples, Spain, and Portugal, the congresses at Troppau, Laibach, and Verona authorized intervention.

Rebellion and revolution

After Greek revolt against Ottoman rule, Greece was declared a sovereign state by 1822, but Turkish forces, bolstered by Egyptian troops, invaded in 1825. The conservative nature of the Greek rebellion, combined with strategic machinations against the crumbling Ottoman empire, led the European powers to approve an autonomous Greek state. A British, French, and Russian naval force destroyed the Turkish–Egyptian fleet at Navarino, and the Ottomans conceded Greek independence in 1832. Revolutions in Modena, Parma, the Papal States, Poland, and parts of Germany broke out in 1830–31, but were all suppressed. Charles X's regime in France was ended by the July Revolution of 1830, though this led not to a new republic but to the accession of the "citizen-king," Louis-Philippe.

The rise of republics

After February 1848, when Louis-Philippe's regime fell to republicans, unrest spread and liberal governments were installed in Hungary, Croatia, and the Czech lands. Republics were proclaimed throughout Italy and a parliamentary assembly met with the aim of uniting Germany. Yet internal divisions prevailed, and by late 1849 the Habsburgs regained control in Austria, Italy, and Hungary; the German assembly collapsed under pressure from Prussia, which consolidated its power by means of victories over Denmark, Austria, and France.

Forming a united Italy

Since 1820 revolutionary movements in Italy, such as the Carbonari, had failed to expel the Austrians. In 1859 the Piedmontese king Victor Emmanuel II and his prime minister Camillo di Cavour instituted liberal domestic reforms and with the help of Napoleon III's France drove the Austrians from Italy. The liberal constitutional monarchy sought by Piedmont was threatened when revolutionary "Redshirts" led by Giuseppe Garibaldi took Sicily and the southern mainland. Yet Garibaldi passed his conquests to Emmanuel, who effectively became king of a united Italy in 1870.

British and Irish nationalism

In Britain the Chartists sought universal male suffrage after limited parliamentary reform was conceded in 1832. Irish nationalism was given urgency by the famine of 1845–47, and the Irish Republican Brotherhood (Fenians), precursor of the movement that won Irish independence in 1921, formed in 1858.

Curriculum Context

Students studying nationalism in Europe should focus on the movements to unify Germany and Italy.

Chartists

Group of mainly working class people who supported the "People's Charter," a six-point plan for constitutional reforms.

The Industrial Revolution

The Industrial Revolution spread from Britain across the rest of Europe, and the newly mechanized industries spurred rapid urban growth and economic development.

Legend:

border, 1914

heavy industrial or mining area

major textile manufacturing area

other large coal deposit

other large iron ore deposit

urban population, 1914

● under 100,000

■ 100,000–500,000

▣ 500,000–1,000,000

◆ over 1,000,000

oilfield, 1914

port

center of socialism

Berlin research and development center for the chemical industry

19m national population (million) where known, 1914

railroad constructed by 1870

railroad constructed 1870–1914

Map labels:

Lake Onega

Lake Ladoga

Vyborg

Helsinki

Narva

Revel

St Petersburg

Lake Peipus

Riga

Libau

Memel

Western Dvina

Königsberg

Vilna

Minsk

RUSSIAN EMPIRE
171m

Warsaw

dz

Kiev

Dnieper

Krakow

Lvov (Lemberg)

Dniester

AUSTRO-HUNGARIAN EMPIRE
51m

dapest

Szeged

Odessa

Ploiesti

Bucharest

Danube

ROMANIA
7.1m

Black Sea

Belgrade

Varna

SERBIA
3.2m

Sofia

BULGARIA
4.3m

MONTENEGRO
0.6m

Edirne

Constantinople

Ankara

ANATOLIA

ALBANIA

Thessalonica

OTTOMAN EMPIRE

GREECE

Izmir

Konya

Athens

Rhodes

Crete

Damascus

Acre

Jerusalem

Vistula

The Industrial Revolution

From the last quarter of the 18th century to the outbreak of World War I in 1914, Europe transformed from a series of traditional agrarian communities into modern industrial nations. The widespread adoption of capitalism, the factory system, and mechanization led to a period of unparalleled economic growth, interrupted by cyclical depressions.

There was also a rapid increase in population and an influx of people from the countryside into the towns and cities that sprang up around the new workplaces.

The workshop of the world

The Industrial Revolution, as this transformation came to be known, had its origins in Britain. Its effects were first seen in the cotton and woollen industries in the north of the country. Mechanical innovations improved the speed and efficiency of weaving, and required new factories powered first by waterwheels and later by steam engines. These factories brought together the various operations involved in textile manufacture. Britain was ideally placed to pioneer and develop mass production, possessing abundant natural resources to power the new machinery, favorable terrain on which to construct extensive transport networks (canals in the late 18th and early 19th centuries, and rail from the 1830s onward), and a ready market for manufactured goods. By 1815, Britain's industrialists had already made it the "workshop of the world," with coal mining, textile production, and pig-iron smelting exceeding the output of the rest of Europe combined.

The spread of industrialization

Industrialization had spread to mainland Europe by the end of the 18th century (for example, in the Belgian armaments industry or cotton weaving in Saxony and northern France), but Britain's embargo on the emigration of skilled artisans and the export of machinery during the Napoleonic period prevented a wider adoption of the new methods of production. Beginning in the 1820s in Belgium, however, coal mining and the textile and metal industries took root in continental Europe. As in Britain, the new rail network played a major role in promoting economic expansion; rail transportation allowed rapid distribution of goods and its consumption of materials stimulated further growth. By 1890 nearly all the main rail routes across Europe had been completed.

Financing the Industrial Revolution

Private investment lay behind the success of many major industrial ventures, such as some early railroads, but spectacular bankruptcies showed the need for a new method of funding capital projects. Especially in continental Europe, joint-stock limited liability companies, supported by development banks, were founded to provide credit. Free trade was another crucial factor in industrial expansion. Britain lifted its high import duties on corn in 1846; agreements with France, the Prussian Zollverein, and Belgium in the 1860s further encouraged the reduction of tariffs. By 1870 most European countries had expanded foreign trade and industrial production by lowering or abolishing their tariffs—though the position gradually reversed after the Franco-Prussian War (1870–71).

Social effects

The social effects of the Industrial Revolution were as radical as its technological and financial consequences. The years of growth between 1840–70 also witnessed periodic financial crises and bouts of widespread unemployment. Harvests were critical, causing wild fluctuations in the price of food. Later, the import of cheap foodstuffs from Canada, the United States, and Russia undercut agriculture in the industrializing states. New production methods

Curriculum Context

There are important connections between Britain's early industrialization and its commercial relations with continental Europe and other world regions.

Free trade

The abolition of import tariffs protecting local producers from competition.

Curriculum Context

An important aspect of industrialization and urbanization is the effect it had on class distinctions, family life, and the daily working lives of men, women, and children.

threatened traditional skills, sometimes leading to machine-wrecking by disgruntled workers. As mechanization spread, working conditions became more hazardous. Employers exploited the large pool of child and female labor to depress wages. Living conditions deteriorated in the vastly expanding new cities, where sanitation failed to keep pace with population growth. Cholera and typhus epidemics were common. A second bout of industrialization after 1870, based on steel and the new power source of electricity, did little to alleviate these problems.

Child labor was common in the mines of early 19th-century Britain, but was banned in 1842.

Curriculum Context

The ideas of Karl Marx and Marxist beliefs and programs had an important impact on politics, industry, and labor relations in later 19th-century Europe.

Early trade unions

To challenge the effects of capital, both the industrial working classes and the rural peasantry (serfdom did not end in Russia until 1861) organized themselves into trade unions. These efforts met opposition from the state as well as the capitalists. Ideas for alternative ways of structuring society arose during this period. Socialist parties were formed to argue for a more equal distribution of wealth, becoming particularly strong in Germany and France. Karl Marx and Friedrich Engels published their *Communist Manifesto* in 1848, arguing for a class-based revolution in highly industrialized states such as Britain. Anarchists advocated the violent abolition of the state, while syndicalists sought worker-control of industry through general strikes. To forestall social upheaval, some governments enacted legislation to alleviate the worst effects of industrialization. Compulsory free state education was widely instituted; labor in factories and mines was gradually regulated and child labor banned; working hours were cut and wages rose (as did inflation); improved housing also became slowly available. The first decade of the 20th century was marked by widespread unrest, but the old problem of unemployment would be briefly answered by the demands of World War I.

Curriculum Context

It may be useful to understand the connections between industrialization and the rise of new types of labor organizations and mobilization.

Poverty and Unemployment

For many people, the solution to poverty was to emigrate. Nearly half a million Poles moved west to find jobs in the industrialized Ruhr, and Italian farmers took harvest work in Germany, France, and Austria. Yet far more people left Europe, emigrating in their millions to Australia and New Zealand, but above all to the Americas.

European Alliances

At the end of the 19th century, nations formed alliances with one another to maintain the balance of power across Europe and prevent warfare.

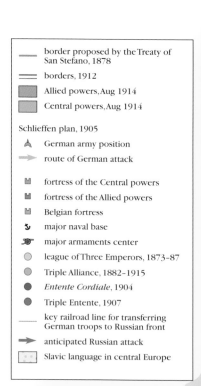

N

N o
S

Scapa Flow

Cromarty

Glasgow · Rosyth
Edinburgh

Belfast

UNITED KINGDOM
Dublin ·

Birmingham ·

Ams
Harwich
Chatham
Bristol · London · Anty
Portsmouth BEL
Plymouth · Portland Boulogne
Cherbourg La Fère
Rouen · Laon
· Brest Paris

Lorient Orléans
Loire Le Creusc
· Nantes FRANC

Rochefort

Lye
Bordeaux · G

La Coruña Santander
Bilbao Toulouse Mar

ANDORRA
Douro
Oporto Zaragoza
Ebro
SPAIN Barcelona
Madrid ·
PORTUGAL Tagus
Valencia · Balearic
· Lisbon Guadiana Islands

Córdoba · · Alicante
· Seville
Cádiz · Algiers
Algeçiras · Gibraltar
Tangier to Britain
Spanish Morocco
1912 Spanish protectorate

Legend

— border proposed by the Treaty of San Stefano, 1878

= borders, 1912

■ Allied powers, Aug 1914

■ Central powers, Aug 1914

Schlieffen plan, 1905

⚑ German army position

→ route of German attack

🏰 fortress of the Central powers

🏰 fortress of the Allied powers

🏰 Belgian fortress

⚓ major naval base

⚙ major armaments center

○ league of Three Emperors, 1873–87

○ Triple Alliance, 1882–1915

● *Entente Cordiale*, 1904

● Triple Entente, 1907

— key railroad line for transferring German troops to Russian front

→ anticipated Russian attack

▫ Slavic language in central Europe

NORWAY

Christiania

SWEDEN

Stockholm

Göteborg

Vänern

Vättern

Gotland

Baltic Sea

Helsinki

Revel

Lake Ladoga

St Petersburg

Lake Peipus

Riga

Western Dvina

DENMARK

Copenhagen

Kiel Canal

Kiel

Hamburg

Bremen

en

Memel

Kovno

Vilna

Minsk

Danzig

Königsberg

Grodno

RUSSIAN EMPIRE

the

Stettin

Thorn

Poznan

GERMAN EMPIRE

Berlin

Hanover

Leipzig

Dresden

Breslau

Glatz

Oder

Warsaw

Brest-Litovsk

Ivangorod

Frankfurt

BOURG

enhofen

Neuenburg

sbourg

f-Brisach

Prague

Pilsen

AUSTRO–HUNGARIAN EMPIRE

Krakow

Vistula

Przemysl

Lemberg

Ingolstadt

Munich

Salzburg

Danube

Vienna

Komorn

Budapest

Odessa

RLAND

Trent

LIECHTENSTEIN

Karlsburg

Sevastopol

Milan

Venice

Trieste

Pola

1878 occupied by Austria–Hungary, 1908 annexed by Austria–Hungary

Sava

Peterwardein

Belgrade

ROMANIA independent 1878

Bucharest

Black Sea

Bologna

SAN MARINO

Bosnia–Herzegovina

Sarajevo

SERBIA independent 1878

Aleksinac 1876

Danube

NACO

Florence

MONTENEGRO

Mostar

1913 to Montenegro

Pleven 1877

BULGARIA independent 1908

Varna

ITALY

Rome

Trebinje

Cattaro

Kumanovo 1912

Sofia

East Rumelia 1885 to Bulgaria

1913 to Serbia

1913 to Greece

Edirne

Kirk Kilisse 1912

1913 to Bulgaria

Constantinople

Albania independent 1913

Thessalonica

San Stefano

Lüleburgaz 1912

ANATOLIA

Naples

Taranto

Ionian Islands

GREECE

OTTOMAN EMPIRE

Palermo

Messina

Sicily

Athens

Tunis

Rhodes

Dodecanese 1912 to Italy

Cyprus 1878 to Britain

Tunisia 71 autonomous, 1881 French protectorate

Malta to Britain

Crete 1898 autonomous, 1908 to Greece

Mediterranean Sea

Port Said

Suez Canal built 1859–69

Alexandria

Cairo

EGYPT 1882 British protectorate

European Alliances

German chancellor Otto von Bismarck, who initiated the complex web of alliances that developed after the Franco–Prussian War (1870–71), now had as his ultimate objective the preservation of peace on the continent. He aimed to prevent France from launching a war of revenge by isolating it from any potential ally.

Dreikaiserbund

Alliance of Germany, Austria-Hungary, and Russia. It aimed to neutralize the rivalry between Germany's two neighbors and to isolate Germany's enemy, France.

Bismarck's first step was to form the league of Three Emperors (*Dreikaiserbund*) between Germany, Austria–Hungary, and Russia in 1873. In doing so, he had to reconcile a number of conflicting interests. Since the Crimean War, Russia had tried to reassert its position in Europe by championing the cause of Slav freedom from Austrian and Turkish rule. This brought Austria and Russia into conflict, as both empires cherished ambitions to secure the Balkan lands of the moribund Ottoman empire. The loose alliance that Bismarck forged was designed to stabilize southeast Europe, as its signatories agreed to act in concert against subversive movements in the region. In 1878, however, the Congress of Berlin forced Russia to renounce some of the excessive Balkan gains it had wrested from Turkey in 1877–78.

The Triple Alliance

The chief beneficiary of the Berlin Congress was Austria, which negotiated a secret, defensive Dual Alliance with Germany (who, in World War I, were known as the Central Powers). This relationship was to be the main focus of Bismarck's subsequent diplomacy; he publicly renewed the *Dreikaiserbund* in 1881 and distracted France by encouraging its colonial ambitions in north Africa, but secretly created a Triple Alliance between Germany, Austria, and Italy. By forming the Alliance, the three countries agreed to support each other if attacked by either France or Russia.

Curriculum Context

In some states, students are expected to understand how the system of alliances developed by Bismarck was designed to isolate a hostile France and to avoid war in Europe.

Bismarck's diplomacy

When the Dreikaiserbund expired in 1887, Bismarck replaced it with a bilateral Reinsurance Treaty, which recognized the Balkans as a Russian sphere of influence and confirmed that Russia and Germany would stay neutral unless Germany attacked France or Russia attacked Austria. This represented the pinnacle of Bismarck's diplomacy, which sought to secure German predominance in central Europe and avoid dangerous adventurism.

A new military alliance

In 1890, a sea-change occurred in the politics of European alliances, when growing antagonism between the headstrong new emperor Wilhelm II and Bismarck brought the latter's resignation. The Reinsurance Treaty was allowed to lapse without renewal and the Russian harvest failed the same year. France offered aid to Russia, so laying the groundwork for a military alliance. This was duly signed in 1894, with the critical provision that if a Triple Alliance country mobilized its armies then Russia and France would do likewise. Mobilization of any armed forces was thus likely to lead to war.

Curriculum Context

The pattern of alliances and spheres of influence in Europe laid the foundations for the hostile combatants in World War I (1914–18).

Otto von Bismarck was known as the Iron Chancellor for his success at unifying the different German states while managing not to upset Europe's balance of power.

Entente Cordiale

Usually translated as "friendly understanding," the term refers to an agreement between France and Britain to cooperate over colonial interests.

The Triple Entente

Britain had stood aloof from these alliances, but after the death of Queen Victoria in 1901 the new king Edward VII (r.1901–10) made overtures to France that culminated in the Entente Cordiale of 1904. A similar agreement was made with Russia in 1907, forming a Triple Entente (of what became known as the Allied powers in 1914) to balance the Triple Alliance.

European royalty in the early 20th century had close family ties. Britain's King George V (shown here with Queen Mary) was cousin to Wilhelm II of Germany and Tsar Nicholas II of Russia.

Changes in southeast Europe

Several international incidents occurred that tested the commitment of the European powers to peace. Germany's claims to Morocco ran into opposition from both Britain and France, and resulted in the Tangier crisis (1905), settled at the Algeciras conference, and the Agadir crisis of 1911, which resulted in German recognition of France's claim to Morocco. The Balkans, too, continued to provide a highly charged arena. The Balkan peoples tried to organize into nation-states and the Balkan Wars of 1912 and 1913 radically transformed the map of southeast Europe, arousing the hostility of Austria–Hungary.

Developments in the machinery of war

Rapid developments were made in armaments. Germany produced medium and heavy artillery of high quality, France excelled in rapid-fire field guns, while all countries were perfecting the machine-gun. At sea, the British Dreadnought class of battleship, begun in 1906, inaugurated a new era of naval design. Heavily armored, equipped entirely with big guns, and driven by steam turbines, these ships started a race to build ever more powerful fleets. Wilhelm II was especially keen to develop a navy to challenge the might of Britain's Royal Navy.

Plans for war

Throughout this period, plans were made for war. The most ambitious was devised by the German chief of staff, Alfred von Schlieffen, for a war on two fronts. The Schlieffen plan required a rapid push through neutral Holland, Belgium, and Luxembourg to isolate Paris from the coast and encircle the French armies. Troops would then be transferred by rail to reinforce the eastern front against Russia, which was expected to attack near Königsberg.

Mass mobilization

Conscription swelled the size of the continent's armies. Most German youth served for three years in the army corps; French conscripts served for two. Both of these countries (and Italy) could mobilize a million men within days. Austria and Russia could call on three times this number, though more slowly. The threat of war had loomed for so long over Europe that by 1914 all countries had arsenals and forces of unparalleled size and efficiency.

Curriculum Context

Students studying the underlying causes of World War I should consider the relative importance of economic and political rivalries, ethnic and ideological conflicts, militarism, and imperialism.

The Decline of the Ottomans

The Ottoman empire had been at the height of its power in the 16th and 17th centuries, but from the late 18th century the empire began to break up.

N

North Sea

SWEDEN

DENMARK

Baltic Sea

Berlin
Elbe
Oder

GERMAN EMPIRE

NETHERLANDS
BELGIUM

LUXEMBOURG
Karlsruhe
Stuttgart
Vienna
Danube

Paris
Rhine
Munich

Budapest

LIECHTENSTEIN

Loire

FRANCE
SWITZERLAND

SAN MARINO

Bosnia–Herzegovina
1908 to Austro-Hungarian empire
Sarajevo
Sava

MONACO
ITALY
MONTENEGRO
1878 independence renewed

Marseille
Toulon

Corsica
Rome

ALBANIA
1913 independent

ANDORRA

1830

Douro
Ebro

SPAIN
Madrid

1881

Sardinia

Taranto

1911

PORTUGAL

Tagus

Guadiana

Balearic Islands

Sicily

Bizerte
Tunis

Algiers
Bone
Tunisia
1871 autonomous
1881 French protectorate

Malta

Tangier
Gibraltar
to Britain
Oran

1852

Spanish Morocco
1912 Spanish protectorate

Algeria
1830/48 to France

Casablanca
French Morocco
1912 French protectorate

Laghouat

Tripoli

Tripolitania
1912 to Italy

Fezzan
1842 to Ottoman empire

Murzaq

Legend

- Ottoman empire, 1800
- Ottoman territory lost, 1805–1914
- Wahhabi influence
- Wahhabi attack
- "Big Bulgaria" devised by Russia, 1878
- borders, 1914
- Ottoman empire, 1914
- Austro-Hungarian empire, 1914
- British territory, 1914
- British sphere of influence, 1907
- French territory, 1914
- Italian territory, 1914
- Russian empire, 1914
- Russian sphere of influence, 1907
- Spanish territory, 1914
- Turkey, 1923
- revolt or uprising
- known oilfield, 1914
- Orient Express railroad, 1800
- extension of Orient Express to Berlin and Baghdad
- Hejaz railroad
- campaign of Mehmet Ali and Ibrahim
- French campaign
- Italian campaign
- Russian campaign, 1877–78

Dnieper
Bessarabia
Jassy
Moldavia
Odessa
Ochakov
Anapa

RUSSIAN
EMPIRE

CRIMEA

ROMANIA
1878 independent
Bucharest

Sevastopol

CAUCASUS MTS

Derbent

Caspian Sea

Danube

BULGARIA
1908 independent

Black Sea

Sukhumi
Poti
Batum

1784–1878 to
Russian empire

Tbilis

Baku

KUBAN

Kars

Armenia
1828 to Russian
empire

Astara

Svilen
THRACE
Young Turk uprising, 1908

San Stefano
Constantinople
Izmit

Sinope
1853

Nakhichevan

Thessalonica

Macedonia
e 1913 to Greece

ECE
dependent

Athens

arino

ANATOLIA

Ankara

OTTOMAN
EMPIRE

Kutahya

1833

1832 Konya 1832

Nezib
1839

ZAGROS

Euphrates

Tigris

Iraq

PERSIA

MTS

Dodecanese
1912 to Italy

Rhodes

Crete
1878 autonomous
1913 to Greece

Cyprus
1878 to Britain

Syria

1832

Beirut

Damascus

Karbala Baghdad

1802

Acre

LEVANT

Mediterranean Sea

na

Tobruk

Jerusalem

Port Said

Alexandria

Tel el-Kebir

1882

Ismailiya

Suez Canal
built 1859–69

Cairo

Suez

Urabi Pasha
uprising, 1881–82

Cyrenaica
1912 to Italy

EGYPT
1805 autonomous
1882 British protectorate
1922 independent but under
British influence

1811–15

Hejaz

1816–18

Medina

1805

1803

Kuwait
1899 British protectorate

Bandar Abbas

Bahrain
1861 British protectorate

Qatar
1868 British protectorate

EL-HASA

Musc

Trucial Oman
1853 British protectorate

Oman protectorate

1891 British protectorate

Dariya

Riyadh

Wahhabi-influenced
by 1818

Jiddah

Mecca

Red Sea

Asir

Sudan
1898 Anglo–Egyptian
Condominium

Suakin

Arab rulers conduct
foreign relations
through British
representatives, 1892

Hadramaut
1888 British protectorate

YEMEN
1919
independence
renewed

Sana

Eritrea
1889 to Italy

Massawa

West Aden Protectorate
1903 British protectorate

Italian Somaliland
1889 to Italy

ETHIOPIA

French
Somaliland

Aden
1839 to Britain

British Somaliland
1884 to Britain

The Decline of the Ottomans

In the late 18th century the Europeans continued to encroach on the Ottoman empire. In a second war against the Turks (1787–92), Catherine II of Russia failed to partition the Ottoman empire, but still extended Russian control of the northern Black Sea coast.

Further losses were incurred in 1806–12, when Russia gained Bessarabia. Insurrections also broke out in Serbia in 1804 and 1817. Later attempts by the Ottomans to regain control of Serbia and the Principalities (Wallachia and Moldavia) resulted in the Russo-Turkish war of 1828–29, and the concession of Serbian autonomy.

An empire under threat

Yet the most serious threat to the empire's survival during this period came from its vassal state of Egypt. Napoleon's invasion of 1798 profoundly altered Egypt's internal politics: Mehmet Ali, an Albanian officer of the force sent by the Ottoman ruler Sultan Selim III to expel the French, seized control of the state, becoming viceroy in 1805. At first, this dynamic modernizing leader aided the Ottomans, ending the occupation of the Muslim holy sites of Arabia by the fanatical Wahhabi sect and acceding to Sultan Mahmud II's request in 1825 for help in the Greek War of Independence. However, in 1831 Mehmet Ali and his son Ibrahim Pasha (commander of the Egyptian force in Greece) invaded Syria to assert their authority against the sultan.

European aid

Ottoman power was almost broken by defeats in 1832 at Konya in Anatolia, and in 1839 at Nezib (northern Syria), but the empire was saved by the Austrians and the British, who were afraid that a power vacuum in the region would threaten their links with India.

Curriculum Context

Students studying the decline of the Ottoman empire should understand the impact of the French invasion of Egypt in 1798.

Curriculum Context

One notable aspect of the Ottoman decline was the defensive reform programs introduced by Selim III and Mahmud II to resolve the empire's political and economic crises.

Janissaries (Ottoman infantry soldiers) in traditional costume before the corps was abolished in 1826.

Western support increases

Further western support for the Ottomans appeared during the Crimean War. The conflict arose from a Russian claim to protect Orthodox Christians in Ottoman European territories, and was fueled by disagreements between Russia and France over the administration of holy sites in Jerusalem. Russia invaded Moldavia and Wallachia, and in response Turkey (supported by Britain and France) declared war. Turkey's naval defeat at Sinope was followed by British and French assaults on the Crimea. The outcome of the war was a united Romania (in 1861) and an agreement to preserve the diminishing Ottoman empire.

Crimean War

War fought in Crimea, Russia in 1853–56 that arose from British and French mistrust of Russian ambitions in the Balkans.

French and British influences

French influence in the Levant grew after France sent an expedition to Syria in 1860 to halt a massacre of Maronite Christians. France had also gained the concession to build the Suez Canal in 1854 (completed in 1869). However, the debt-ridden khedive (the Ottoman viceroy of Egypt's new title) sold his canal shares to Britain in 1875. Arab nationalists led by Urabi Pasha now began to agitate against European influence in Egyptian affairs. France and Britain gradually adopted a more interventionist approach toward Ottoman survival. France established a protectorate in Tunisia in 1881, and Egypt, nominally still an autonomous viceroyalty of the Ottoman empire, was occupied by Britain.

Balkan rebellions

Nationalist rebellions in Bosnia–Herzegovina, Serbia, Bulgaria, and Montenegro provoked yet another Russian invasion of the Ottoman empire (1877); the ensuing Peace of San Stefano created a pro-Russian "Big Bulgaria." Yet a congress of European powers at Berlin in 1878 revised these frontiers to check Russian expansion. The Ottomans' last foothold in Bulgaria— eastern Rumelia—was lost when this province rebelled and merged with Bulgaria in 1885–88.

German support

In 1898, a surprise visit to Constantinople by Kaiser Wilhelm II consolidated a growing Ottoman association with Germany. Turkey and Germany agreed to extend the Orient Express railroad across Asia Minor to Baghdad. Subsequently Sultan Abdul Hamid II raised Muslim subscriptions to build the Hejaz railroad between Damascus and Medina.

Foreign encroachment

Fears for the continuing demise of the Ottoman empire led disaffected army officers under Enver Pasha—the

"Young Turks"—to overthrow Abdul Hamid in 1909. The reformers promoted westernization, but foreign encroachment began again. Austria annexed Bosnia–Herzegovina in 1908, Italy took Tripolitania in 1912, and two Balkan wars (1912–13) were precipitated, further reducing the Ottoman empire. Apart from eastern Thrace, all the European and north African provinces had now vanished.

The end of the empire

In 1914 Turkey's new rulers staked its future on a secret alliance with Germany. The Treaty of Sèvres (1920), signed upon the defeat of the Central powers, stripped the Ottoman empire of all its non-Turkish regions. After capitulation, a war of independence was waged by nationalists under Kemal Atatürk from 1919–23, which drove foreign forces from Anatolia. In 1923 the Ottoman empire ceased to exist after more than six hundred years.

Annexed

When one territory is taken over, often forcibly, and incorporated into another territory.

J.Albert Adams
Academy Media Center

Africa Before the Scramble

The diversity and influence
of African empires was
profoundly impacted by
the presence of European
colonies and trading across
the continent.

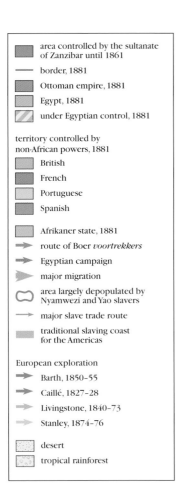

area controlled by the sultanate of Zanzibar until 1861

border, 1881

Ottoman empire, 1881

Egypt, 1881

under Egyptian control, 1881

territory controlled by non-African powers, 1881

British

French

Portuguese

Spanish

Afrikaner state, 1881

route of Boer *voortrekkers*

Egyptian campaign

major migration

area largely depopulated by Nyamwezi and Yao slavers

major slave trade route

traditional slaving coast for the Americas

European exploration

Barth, 1850–55

Caillé, 1827–28

Livingstone, 1840–73

Stanley, 1874–76

desert

tropical rainforest

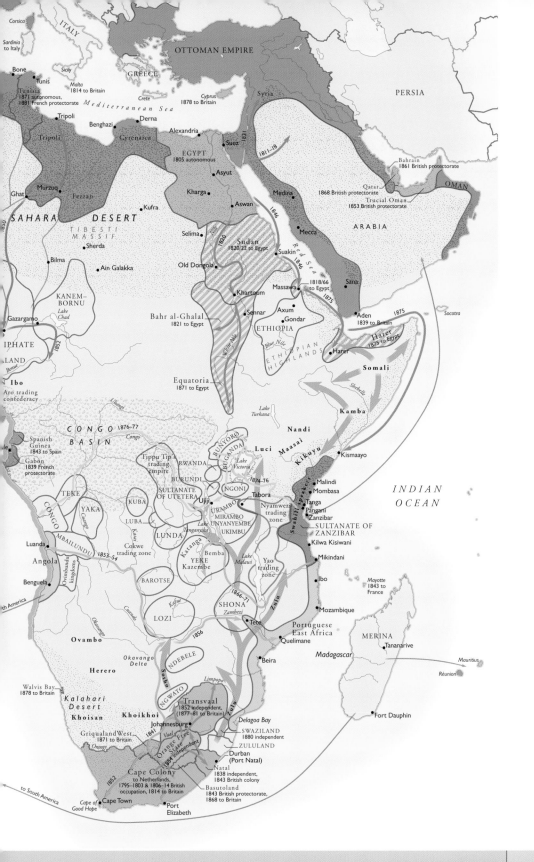

Corsica
to Italy

ITALY

Sardinia
to Italy

Sicily

Bone

Tunis

Tunisia
1871 autonomous,
1881 French protectorate

Malta
1814 to Britain

GREECE

OTTOMAN EMPIRE

Crete

Mediterranean Sea

Cyprus
1878 to Britain

Syria

PERSIA

Tripoli

Benghazi

Derna

Alexandria

1831

Suez

1811–18

Bahrain
1861 British protectorate

Tripoli

Cyrenaica

EGYPT
1805 autonomous

Medina

Qatar
1868 British protectorate

OMAN

Trucial Oman
1853 British protectorate

Ghat

Murzuq

Fezzan

Asyut

Kharga

SAHARA   DESERT

TIBESTI
MASSIF

Sherda

Selima

Aswan

1846

Mecca

ARABIA

Bilma

Ain Galakka

Nile

1820

Sudan
1820/22 to Egypt

Suakin 1846

1818/66
to Egypt

1875

Sana

Aden
1839 to Britain

1875

Socotra

KANEM-
BORNU

*Lake
Chad*

Old Dongola

Massawa

Gazargamo

Khartoum

Sennar

Axum

Gondar

Harer
1875 to Egypt

Harer

IPHATE

1852

Bahr al-Ghalal
1821 to Egypt

ETHIOPIA

Somali

Benue

White Nile

Blue Nile

E T H I O P I A N
HIGHLANDS

Ibo

Aro trading
confederacy

Equatoria
1871 to Egypt

Shebelle

Lake
Turkana

Kamba

C O N G O
B A S I N

1876–77

Ubangi

Nandi

Luci

Maasai

Kikuyu

Kismaayo

Spanish
Guinea
1843 to Spain

Gabon
1839 French
protectorate

Congo

Tippu Tip's
trading
empire

RWANDA

BUNYORO

BUGANDA

Lake
Victoria

1874–76

Malindi

Mombasa

TEKE

YAKA

KUBA

BURUNDI

NGONI

SULTANATE
OF UTETERA

Ujiji

Tabora

Tanga

Pangani

Zanzibar

SULTANATE OF
ZANZIBAR

CONGO

Kwango

LUBA

URAMBO

MIRAMBO

UNYANYEMBE

UKIMBU

Nyamwezi
trading
zone

MBAILUNDU

LUNDA

Kasai

Katanga

*Lake
Tanganyika*

Kilwa Kisiwani

Luanda

Cokwe
trading zone

YEKE
KAZEMBE

Bemba

*Lake
Malawi*

Yao
trading
zone

Mikindani

Angola

1853–54

BAROTSE

Ibo

Mayotte
1843 to
France

Benguela

Ovimbundu
kingdoms

LOZI

Kafue

SHONA

1866–71

Zambezi

Mozambique

Cuanza

Cuando

1856

Tete

Portuguese
East Africa

MERINA

Ovambo

*Okavango
Delta*

NDEBELE

Beira

Quelimane

Tananarive

Madagascar

Mauritius

Herero

Zulu

Okavango

Walvis Bay
1878 to Britain

*Kalahari
Desert*

Khoisan

NGWATO

Limpopo

Delagoa Bay

Fort Dauphin

Réunion

Griqualand West
1871 to Britain

Johannesburg

Transvaal
1852 independent,
(1877–81 to Britain)

SWAZILAND
1880 independent

ZULULAND

Orange

1841

Vaal

Orange Free
State
1854 independent

Durban
(Port Natal)

Cape Colony
to Netherlands,
1795–1803 & 1806–14 to Britain

Natal
1838 independent,
1843 British colony

to South America

1852

Cape of
Good Hope

Cape Town

Port
Elizabeth

Basutoland
1843 British protectorate,
1868 to Britain

INDIAN
OCEAN

Red Sea

Swahili speakers

Africa Before the Scramble

Before the late 19th century European settlement of Africa was mostly confined to French colonization of Algeria, a few Spanish settlements, British and French trading stations in west Africa, and Portuguese trade along the coast. Native peoples offered stern resistance, notably the Asante of west Africa.

Afrikaner

White inhabitant of South Africa descended from Dutch settlers.

Curriculum Context

Students studying 19th-century Africa should be aware of the importance of the rise of the Zulu empire on African societies and European colonial settlement.

The largest European presence was formed by Afrikaner and British settlers in southern Africa, first in Cape Colony and (after the Great Trek, which began in 1835–36) in the Orange Free State and Transvaal. Disruption was caused by population movements, expansion by indigenous states such as Egypt, holy wars (jihads), the slave trade, and the emergence of new empires in east, central, and west Africa.

African rulers

In southern Africa, Shaka, who formed the Zulu kingdom from 1816, initiated a period of expansion. Zulu victories caused a chain-reaction among other nations, which surrendered to the Zulu confederacy or came into conflict with other nations as they fled. In west Africa, Usman dan Fodio aimed to create a unified Muslim state in Hausaland. He established the Sokoto caliphate that survived until the 20th century. To the west, Sheikh Ahmad Lobbo led the Masina jihad; his rival Al Hajj Umar created the Tukulor caliphate. Samori Toure brought order, prosperity, and Islamic law to a diverse set of peoples torn by commercial and religious conflict when he created the First Samori empire.

Slave trading

The trade in slaves was abolished by Denmark, Britain, France, and the United States in the early 19th century, but Portugal allowed it to continue until 1882. Over 50,000 slaves a year were taken from Angola and

Madagascar to South America and (up to 1865) illegally into the United States. The trans-Saharan and east African slave trades also flourished. A permanent settlement of the Omani Arabs in Zanzibar guaranteed a demand for African slaves in the Middle East and Asia, until that market closed in 1873. Many African peoples were involved in the slave trade; the Yao and Nyamwezi, for example, depopulated much of east Africa in search of slaves for their plantations.

Curriculum Context

An influential consequence of the international trade in commodities such as ivory, cloves, and slaves was the rise of Zanzibar and other commercial empires in East Africa.

African state-building

The presence of Muslim slave traders—Swahilis, Arabs, Egyptians, and Sudanese—led to a spate of African state-building. Commercial empires such as Tippu Tip's Sultanate of Utetera emerged, which dealt in slaves and ivory throughout east central Africa. The Nyamwezi formed the trading empires of Urambo, Ukimbu, and Unyanyembe. On the floodplain of the upper Zambezi was the rich Lozi empire, while to the northeast lay Kazembe, a prosperous agricultural state. In Angola Cokwe hunters successfully expanded their ivory exports and developed rubber plantations.

The colonization of a continent

African leaders who had abandoned the slave trade now depended on export of commodities. In west Africa exports of timber, gum, gold, beeswax, ivory, and hides doubled from 1808 to 1880. Everywhere, Africans and Europeans were in conflict over trade and access to raw materials; these rivalries created the conditions for partition. European explorers increased in number and ambition. In 1827–28, the Frenchman René-Auguste Caillé traveled through west Africa, and Scottish missionary David Livingstone journeyed extensively in central and southern Africa from 1840. With the discovery of mineral wealth in southern Africa in the 1870s the "scramble" for Africa heralded a more systematic encroachment; the continent was almost totally colonized by 1900.

Partition

Division of a single country into separate areas with different governments.

Africa and European Empires

At the end of the 19th century European countries were scrambling for a greater share of African territory and its rich resources.

PORTUGAL   SPAI

Tangier
Spanish
Morocco   Ora
Madeira
Fez
French
Morocco
Ifni   Agadir   1912 French
1912 Spanish   protectorate
protectorate

Canary Islands
1912 Spanish   Spanish
protectorate   Sahara

Alg

Tua

1906

Rio de Oro
1884 Spanish
protectorate

Taoudenni

1904

Mauritania

1904

Cape Verde
Islands   St Louis   Kaédi   Timbuktu   Gao
Dakar   Nioro   French W
Senegal   1881–94   1891   1891–94   1895 federation o
Gambia   Kayes   French   reorganise
Fort James   1883   Sudan   Segu   1896
Cacheo   Bamako   Upper
Portuguese Guinea   French   Volta   Sa
Bai Bureh's war   Guinea   Samori's resistance,   1896
Conakry   Samori's   1892–98
Sierra Leone   resistance,   1888–90   Gold   1884
Freetown   1881–92   Coast   Togoland
     Asante   1897   protectorate
   Monrovia   resistance   Kumas
Takoradi   Lomé
LIBERIA   1891   Accra
Ivory   Takoradi
Coast

ATLANTIC
OCEAN

Legend

🔲 Mahdist state, 1881–98

─── border, 1914

territory controlled by non-African powers, 1914
- Belgium
- France
- Germany
- Italy
- Ottoman empire
- Portugal
- Spain
- United Kingdom

European routes of expansion, 1880–1914
- ⇨ Belgian
- ⇨ British
- ⇨ French
- ⇨ German
- ⇨ Italian
- ⇨ Portuguese

- ☼ major African resistance
- 🌴 oasis
- ◇ gold
- ◈ diamonds
- ◆ copper
- ◆ coal
- ─── railroads by 1914

Corsica

Sardinia

ITALY

ALBANIA

SERBIA

BULGARIA

GREECE

Sicily

Malta

Crete

Cyprus

OTTOMAN EMPIRE

Syria

PERSIA

Mediterranean Sea

Bone

Tunis

Tunisia
1881 French
protectorate

1881–82

Tripoli

Benghazi

Derna

Tobruk

Alexandria

Tripolitania
1912 to Italy

Cyrenaica
1912 to Italy

1913

Cairo

Suez

Kuwait
1899 British protectorate

Bahrain

Qatar

Riyadh

Trucial
Oman

Muscat

Ghat

Murzuq

Fezzan

Egypt
1882 British protectorate

Medina

ARABIA

Oman
1891 British
protectorate

SAHARA DESERT

TIBESTI
MASSIF

Tushki
1889

Wadi Halfa

1896

1897–98

1898

Suakin

Mecca

Red Sea

Yemen

Sana

Hadramaut
1888 British
protectorate

West Aden
Protectorate
1903 British protectorate

Socotra
1886 British
protectorate

anrasset

Air

Agadez

Bilma

1906

Rabih resistance,
1892–1900

Zinder

1902

Burmi
1903

French Equatorial Africa

1910 federation of dependencies

Chad

Lake
Chad

1900

1884

1896–98

Dongola

Sudan
1898 Anglo-Egyptian
condominium

Omdurman
1898

Khartoum

1899

1898

Fashoda

Nile

White Nile

Blue Nile

1900–01

Massawa

Adowa
1896

Eritrea
1889 to Italy

Aden

French
Somaliland
1884/5 French
protectorate

Djibouti

British Somaliland
1884 British
protectorate

Addis Ababa

ETHIOPIA

Shebelle

Ubangi Shari

Ubangi

Cameroon
1884 to Germany

Douala

1884

Congo

1896–98

Gabon
to French
Equatorial
Africa

ille

Brazzaville

Leopoldville

Cabinda
6 to Angola

Middle
Congo

Belgian Congo
(Congo Free State)
1885 to Leopold II,
1908 to Belgium as Belgian Congo

Kasai

Kwango

Luanda

Benguela

Angola
1886–90 borders
determined by treaties

Cuanza

Lake
Turkana

Uganda
1894 British
protectorate

Entebbe

Lake
Victoria

Kisuma

British East Africa
1895 British protectorate

Nandi, Embu and
Kisii resistance

Nairobi

1890

Mogadishu

Italian Somaliland
1889 to Italy

INDIAN
OCEAN

Ujiji

Abushiri's
resistance

Tanga

Mombasa

Pemba
1885 to Germany,
1890 to Britain

German
East Africa
1885 to Germany

Pangani

Dar es Salaam

Zanzibar
1885 to Germany,
1890 to Britain

Kitopi

Maji-Maji
rebellion,
1905–07

Kilwa Kisiwani

Lake
Tanganyika

Comoros
1886 to France

Lake
Malawi

Northern Rhodesia
1911 to Britain

Lusaka

Zambezi

Tete

Nyasaland
1891 British
protectorate

Mozambique

Madagascar
1885 French protectorate,
1896 French colony

Tananarive

1894

Mauritius

Réunion

Herero
rebellion,
1904–08

German South-
West Africa
1884 to Germany

Okavango
Delta

Boundary war,
1896

Bechuanaland
1885 British protectorate

Livingstone

Salisbury

1896–1903

Southern Rhodesia
1888 British protectorate

Bulawayo

1896

Limpopo

Beira
1891–94 borders
determined by treaties,
1907 Portuguese colony

Quelimane

Mozambique

Madagascar

1894–1906

Fort Dauphin

Walvis Bay
o Union of South Africa

Nama
rebellion,
1905–09

Windhoek

Mafeking

Johannesburg

Lourenço Marques
Delagoa Bay

Swaziland
1905 British
protectorate

Lüderitz

Bondels–Warts
rebellion, 1904

Kimberley

Vaal

Bambata's rebellion,
1906–08

Durban

UNION OF
SOUTH AFRICA
1910 British dominion

Orange

Basutoland
1843 British
protectorate,
1868 to Britain

Cape Town

Port Elizabeth

Cape of
Good Hope

1911

Africa and European Empires

In 1884–85 representatives of 15 European nations met in Berlin to settle rival claims to Africa. The Berlin Conference did not designate specific regions as colonies; rather it established the broad principles of the large-scale European encroachment that became known as the "scramble for Africa."

Sphere of influence
The hinterland of a coast occupied by a European power.

A power had to show itself capable of protecting "existing rights" and "freedom of trade and transit" to claim a sphere of influence. This doctrine of "effective occupation" meant the process of colonization was violent. Although the partition of Africa was swift, it was the climax of years of activity by traders, administrators, soldiers, and missionaries.

The commercial approach

Some European governments worked through commercial ventures such as the Portuguese Niassa Company and the British South Africa Company. By imposing western practices—abolishing existing currencies, introducing hut taxes, and removing middlemen from established trade patterns—companies like these sowed the seeds of confrontation and armed resistance.

Curriculum Context

Students studying European conquest in Africa should consider the sources and effectiveness of military, political, and religious resistance movements in such regions as the Sudan, Ethiopia, and South Africa.

Labor and resistance

To pay the new taxes, Africans had to undertake wage labor on railroads, rubber, sugar, and cocoa plantations, and mining operations. By forcing Africans into these jobs, Europeans took away their independence and culture . Some—such as the Bugandans who helped the British take over the states that formed Uganda in 1903—collaborated with the invaders. Others put their faith in religion: in the Sudan, Muhammad Ahmed (the Mahdi) rebelled against Anglo-Egyptian rule and founded an Islamic state. Artillery and rapid-fire maxim guns brought most uprisings to a swift end: the Ijebu surrendered in 1892, the Matabele in 1896, the Mandinka (under Toure) in 1898, and the Zulu in 1908.

Exploiting a continent

By 1914, virtually the whole continent had come under European control. African raw materials and human resources were exploited for the benefit of European industry and commerce. Portugal shipped thousands of indentured laborers to cocoa plantations on São Tomé and Príncipe, to live and die in appalling conditions. Leopold II of Belgium, who took the Congo Free State as his personal possession in 1885, amassed a fortune in revenues from rubber and ivory. By 1908 when the Belgian state annexed the Congo, its population was half what it had been in 1891. After this, conditions improved marginally, but thousands of people were moved forcibly to work the copper mines.

Indentured

When a person is voluntarily or involuntarily contracted to work for an employer for a fixed number of years.

Scramble for Africa

With footholds in the west, south, and north of Africa, Britain was well placed to acquire half of the new colonies and protectorates during the "scramble." Its Gold Coast colony was the world's top rubber producer by 1895 and became world leader in cocoa by 1914. Germany came late to colonization. Among its African possessions was Togoland, where medical reforms, support for missionary schools, new roads, and rail links brought some benefits of modern life.

Curriculum Context

It might be useful to consider the scramble for Africa in the context of increased output of European manufactured goods and European desire for new markets.

Defiant nations

The Swazi branch of the Zulu nation was never defeated in battle; their state was guaranteed independence by the Transvaal and the British, before becoming a British protectorate in 1905. Only one state successfully defied the Europeans:

Ethiopia, led by a modernizing Emperor Menelik II, crushed the Italian army at the Battle of Adowa in 1896. The freed-slave state of Liberia also survived despite losing parts of its territory to Britain and France.

Australia and New Zealand

From the late 18th century British settlers began to establish colonies in first Australia and later New Zealand.

Timor Sea

Melville Island
Port
Darwin
Arnhe
Kathe

Wyndham

Kimberley Plateau

Broome

Fitzroy

Northe
(part of South

Port Hedland
Roebourne

Great Sandy Desert

Ashburton

AU
1901 federaliz
as Common
beco

MACDONNE
RANGES

Gibson Desert

Western Australia
founded 1829
1890 self-governing

Murchison

Mount Magnet

Great Victoria Desert

Geraldton

South
found
1855 sel

Menzies

Kalgoorlie

Nullarbor Plain

Perth
Fremantle
Northam
Bunbury
Pinjara
1834

Great Australian Bight

Esperance

Albany

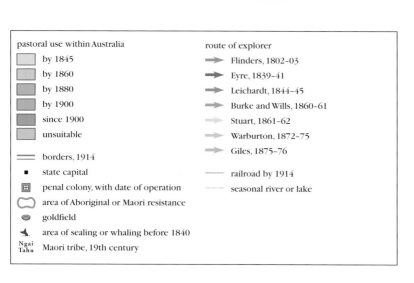

pastoral use within Australia	route of explorer
by 1845	Flinders, 1802–03
by 1860	Eyre, 1839–41
by 1880	Leichardt, 1844–45
by 1900	Burke and Wills, 1860–61
since 1900	Stuart, 1861–62
unsuitable	Warburton, 1872–75
	Giles, 1875–76

borders, 1914

state capital — railroad by 1914

penal colony, with date of operation — — — seasonal river or lake

area of Aboriginal or Maori resistance

goldfield

area of sealing or whaling before 1840

Ngai Tahu — Maori tribe, 19th century

Papua
1884 to Britain
1906 to Australia

Port Moresby

Cape York

Coral Sea

Gulf of Carpentaria

Cooktown

Cairns

urketown Normanton
           Croydon

Townsville

Hughenden   Mackay

GREAT DIVIDING RANGE

Winton

Emerald   Rockhampton
          Mount Morgan

Queensland
founded 1859
1859 self-governing

Bundaberg
Maryborough

Charleville   Toowoomba
              Brisbane
              Moreton Bay
              (1824–42)

Cunnamulla

Marree

Bourke   Inverell

New South Wales
founded 1788
1855 self-governing

Port Macquarie
1821–36

Port Stephens

Broken Hill

Dubbo   Myall
Wellington Creek   Newcastle
            1838×   1804–23

Menindee

Peterborough

Bathurst   Sydney (Port Jackson)
             1788–1840

Botany Bay

Hay   Castle Hill Rising
                 1804

Adelaide

Lambing Flat   Goulburn
               Canberra

Kingston   Albury

Tasman Sea

Bendigo   Victoria
Ballarat founded 1851
          1855 self-governing
          Melbourne

Portland Port Phillip
          1802–52   Western Port
Warrnambool

Bass Strait   *Flinders Island*

Port Dalrymple

Tasmania
founded 1825
1855 self-governing   Launceston

Macquarie Harbour   *Maria Island*
1821–34   1825–32
Hobart
1804–53   Port Arthur
           1830–77
Van Diemen's Land
(renamed Tasmania 1853)

SOUTH PACIFIC OCEAN

Norfolk Island
1788–1814,
1825–1856

Ohaeawai
1845   Russell
Waitangi   Bay of Islands
                       Ngapuhi
North Island

Auckland   Thames
center of
"King Movement"   Waikato

Ngati Toa
Ngati Raukawa
New Plymouth   Gisborne
Te Ati Awa   Napier

NEW ZEALAND
1814 to Britain   Wanganui
1907 British dominion
            Ngati Toa   Palmerston North
Te Ati Awa   Te Ati Awa

Westport   Nelson
            Wellington
Greymouth   Ngati
            Toa

South Island
            Christchurch
            Lyttelton

Queenstown   Cromwell

OTAGO
Ngai
Tahu   Dunedin

Stewart Island   Invercargill

0   600 km
0   400 mi

Australia and New Zealand

European settlement in Australia began when the British government, faced with severe overcrowding in its jails, resolved in 1786 to found a penal colony there. The first convict transports arrived at Botany Bay in 1788; prisoners were subsequently transferred to settlements at Sydney (Port Jackson) and on Norfolk Island.

The young colony began to expand as discharged soldiers and freed convicts cultivated their own parcels of land. Conflict arose with the Aboriginal inhabitants, whose raids on settlements brought reprisals culminating in the massacre of Myall Creek (1838). In the 1830s settlers on Van Diemen's Land (Tasmania) attempted a wholesale expulsion of Aboriginals to Flinders Island; those who resisted were massacred. The free Swan River colony established at Perth and Fremantle in the west attracted over a thousand people by 1831; again, hostilities developed with local peoples. The British government helped sustain the western Australian colony with convict labor until the practice was discontinued in 1868. By then, some 160,000 prisoners had been transported.

Population and governance

The nonconvict populace of Australia rose after 1851, when gold was found at Bathurst, Ballarat, Bendigo, and Kalgoorlie. In 10 years the population exceeded one million; it doubled during the next decade with an influx of Chinese and Asian indentured labor. Racial violence led to strict immigration laws (later emulated in New Zealand). Gold mining played a role in Australian political history: in 1854, the pro-democratic Eureka uprising by Ballarat miners was put down by troops. All the states were self-governing by 1890, and in 1891, Australia's population topped three million, nearly a third of them first-generation immigrants.

Settling New Zealand

European settlers first arrived in New Zealand's Bay of Islands during 1792, exchanging muskets with the indigenous Maoris for land. This trade caused "musket wars" between Maori tribes from 1818. Australian whalers also established coastal settlements on South Island. Disputes between the Maoris and the settlers led to the Treaty of Waitangi, which confirmed the Maoris' right to their land. However, settlers soon violated its terms, and the First Maori War (1843–48) saw fierce fighting. Maori unity appeared in the "King Movement" of 1858 and then in the "Fire in the Fern," a guerrilla war that began in 1860. However, resistance died out, and peace was formally concluded by 1881.

Immigration incentives

Discovery of gold in Otago in 1861 stimulated immigration to New Zealand, but the main incentives to emigrate there and to Australia were cheap shipping fares and high standards of living, including a minimum wage and good welfare benefits. Both countries were enriched by the export of wool and foodstuffs; the introduction of refrigerated holds on steamships in 1882 enabled the bulk transportation of meat and dairy products. Both countries gained self-government when Australia became a Commonwealth in 1901 and New Zealand a Dominion in 1907. Both retained emotional ties with Britain, and sent forces to aid the "mother country" in 1914.

Curriculum Context

Encounters between European colonists and native peoples in such regions as the United States, Australia, and New Zealand were different experiences in each case.

Transcontinental communication

A transcontinental telegraph system was quickly established in Australia, although deserts and mountain ranges presented obstacles to a railroad system and different gauges were adopted by different states. The Trans-Australia Railroad was completed in 1912–17. New Zealand's railroads were also slow to develop. Christchurch and Invercargill were linked in 1880, and regular passenger services began between Wellington and Auckland in 1908.

The Decline of Manchu China

The Manchu dynasty was weakened and finally destroyed by widespread internal rebellion and by foreign influence and invasions.

Omsk•

Toms•

RUSSIAN EMPIRE

Lake
Balkhash

Ili
1854 annexed by Russia
DZUNGARIA

1871–81
to Russia

TIEN SHAN

Tarim

Xinjiang

KUNLUN MTS

TIBET
1912 independent

Manchu empire, mid-19th century

former Manchu tributary state

British India, mid-19th century

Japanese empire, mid-19th century

Russian empire, mid-19th century

borders, c.1912

Manchu /Chinese empire, 1912

former Manchu state gaining independence

Manchu territory lost to Britain by 1912

Manchu territory lost to France by 1912

Manchu territory under Japanese control
at some time before 1912

Manchu territory lost to Russian empire by 1912

temporary Russian territorial gain

area leased by China to foreign power

spheres of influence

British

French

German

Japanese

port open to foreign trade under the
Treaty of Nanjing, 1842

treaty port opened from 1858

Taiping marches, 1850–64

anti-Manchu rebellion, with date

center of Boxer Uprising, 1900–01

railroad by 1914

Trans-Siberian railroad sector completed in 1915

Trans-Siberian rail link to Vladivostok,
completed 1916

Trans-Siberian railroad

completed 1916

completed 1915

Nikolayevsk
founded 1850

Amur
1858 annexed by Russia

Sakhalin
1875 to Russia,
1905 southern half
to Japan

Irkutsk

Chita

Nerchinsk

Aigun

Khabarovsk
founded 1858

Kuril Islands

1875 northern islands to Japan

Lake
Baykal

Manzhouli

Manchuria
1900–05 under Russian influence,
1905–45 under Japanese influence

Ussuri
1860 annexed by Russia

Hokkaido

Sapporo

Ulan Bator

Inner Mongolian
Plateau

Harbin

Suifenhe

Lake
Khanka

Hakodate

MONGOLIA
1912 independent

Changchun

Hunchun

Vladivostok
founded 1860

Sea of
Japan

Gobi Desert

Mukden
(Shenyang)

Niuzhuang

Dandong

KOREA
1905 Japanese protectorate,
1910 Japanese colony

Honshu

Kwangtung Territory
1898–1905 to Russia,
1905 to Japan

Ordos
Desert

Beijing
capital city,
focus of Boxer
Uprising

Qinhuangdao

Yalu River
1894

Tokyo

Yokohama

JAPAN

Ganzhou

Pingluo

Yulin

Shanxi

Hegang

Tianjin

Lushun
(Port Arthur)

Dengzhou

Longkou

Dalian

Weihaiwei
1895

Chefoo

Seoul

Pusan

Shimonoseki

Shikoku

Hezhou

Jinan

Qingdao
1898 to
Germany

Qingdao

Weihaiwei
1898 to Britain

Nagasaki

Kyushu

Lake
Qinghai

Muslim rebellion
1862–73

Nian rebellion
1853–68

Yellow
Sea

Kagoshima

Henan

Yanguan

MPERIAL CHINA

DABA MTS

Huai

Nanjing

Zhenjiang

Shanghai

Wuhu

Hankou

Wuhan

Hangzhou

Suzhou

Wanxian

Yichang

Lichuan

Shasi

Wuchang

Anqing

Taiping
rebellion
1850–64

Ningbo
(Mingzhou)

Mingshan

Chongqing

Yeyang

Jiujiang

Taiping
rebellion
1850–64

Luzhou

Nanchang

Lake
Pengli

Wenzhou

Mianning

Lake
Dongting

Tanzhou

Santuao

Guizhou

Miao rebellion
1855–57

Taiping
rebellion
1850–64

Fuzhou

Tan-shui

Upper Burma
1886 annexed by Britain

Dali

Muslim
rebellion
1855–73

Xiamen
(Amoy)

Aboriginal
rebellion
1862–63

Tengyueh

Yunnan

Hakka rebellion
1855–57

Tainan

Mengzi

Jintian

Wuzhou

Guangzhou
(Canton)

Pescadores
1895 to Japan

Manhao

Nanning

Sanshui

Shantou
(Swatow)

Taiwan
1895 to Japan

Simao

Linan

Longzhou

Kowloon

Tongking
1884–85 French protectorate

Langson

Pakhoi

Macao
to Portugal

Hong Kong

Hanoi

Zhanjiang

Hong Kong
1841 to Britain

Laos
1899 French
protectorate

Burma
1862

Qiongzhou

Hainan

Zhanjiang
1898 to France

Philippine Islands
1571–1898 to Spain,
1898 to United States

South
China
Sea

FRENCH
INDO-CHINA
1887–98 united by
France

Annam
1883–85 French
protectorate

SIAM

Manila

The Decline of Manchu China

Under the expansionist Manchu (Qing) dynasty, China enjoyed unrivaled power in east Asia. By 1783, emperor Qianlong (r.1736–96) had settled colonists in Xinjiang and imposed tributary status on Burma and Annam. He restricted foreign merchants to Guangzhou and shunned the industrial innovations offered by western "barbarian" traders.

Curriculum Context

An important aspect of the decline of Manchu China is the way the opium trade contributed to European penetration of Chinese markets.

After his abdication, imports of opium from British India increased steadily, leading to two "Opium Wars" with China (1839–42; 1856–60). The outcome of the first was the 1842 Treaty of Nanjing, which confirmed Britain's gain of Hong Kong and right to trade through treaty ports; the second resulted in agreements (1858 and 1860) for more western commercial footholds.

Chinese concessions

Russian forces annexed the valuable Ili region and eastern Siberia (1858–60). Britain annexed Burma in 1886. France, entrenched in southern Indo-China, was anxious to open trade with the southern Chinese province of Yunnan and fought a brief war with China to establish a protectorate over Tongking by 1885. Between 1875 and 1880, Japan annexed the Chinese tributary of the Ryukyu islands and began to weaken Chinese influence in another tributary, Korea. China lost Taiwan and the Pescadores in 1894–95. These concessions and defeats represented unprecedented humiliation for the Qing dynasty.

Curriculum Context

The way in which internal problems caused governmental breakdown and social disintegration underlies all of Chinese history in the late 18th century.

Internal issues

China also faced great dangers from within. Official corruption, high taxation, and internal migration caused local uprisings. Many were caused by secret societies. The White Lotus sect vowed to overthrow the Qing and restore the Ming dynasty; their rebellion raged through central China 1796–1804. After 1850 these revolts threatened the survival of the Qing. Hong Xiuquan led the Taiping rebellion, proclaiming the end of Manchu rule. This insurrection and its suppression by Qing forces cost up to 20 million lives. Disaffection with Manchu rule also brought rebellion in Taiwan, Muslim revolts in Xinjiang and Yunnan, Nian peasant risings in Henan, and Miao tribal unrest in Guizhou.

Chinese nationalism

During the reign of the empress Cixi (r.1862–1908), the western clamor for land concessions, mining rights, railroad, and building and trade facilities continued. Anti-western sentiment crystallized into the nationalist movement led by Sun Yixian (Sun Yat-sen). The shame of further territory losses in 1898 led to the Boxer Uprising of 1900–01. The outcome of this rebellion, which was supported by Cixi, was the International Protocol of 1901, which gave the powers more trade concessions and a huge indemnity payment from the Qing. Western soldiers guarded civilian settlements and gunboats patrolled the rivers. Merchant and missionary activity increased, and foreign banks virtually ran China's economy.

Republican revolution

In 1911, Sun Yixian's Revolutionary Alliance Party, or Guomindang (KMT), seized power in central and southern China and overthrew the Qing dynasty. Sun Yixian proclaimed Three Principles of the republican revolution—nationalism, democracy, and people's livelihood—and was appointed provisional president of China. On January 1, 1912, the Chinese Republic was founded. Yet, when the Manchu boy-emperor Pu Yi abdicated on February 13, General Yuan Shikai was named president. For the sake of national unity, Sun had relinquished the presidency. Yet Yuan Shikai's desire to found a new imperial dynasty led him to suppress the KMT. In 1913, Sun Yixian formed the first of a series of provisional governments at Guangzhou.

Curriculum Context

Students studying the Taiping rebellion should focus on its causes and its consequences for the Qing dynasty.

Boxer Uprising

Major revolt by nationalists known as "boxers" that engulfed several provinces but concentrated on attacking the foreign legations in Beijing.

Japan in the 19th Century

In the 19th century Japan
built up its industries and
armed forces to become
a great power, which went
on to control several
neighboring countries.

Irkutsk

Lake
Baykal

Chita

Trans-Siberian railroad

RUSSIAN
EMPIRE

Mongolia
1912 independent

N

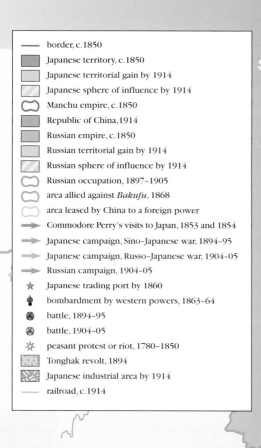

——	border, c.1850
	Japanese territory, c.1850
	Japanese territorial gain by 1914
	Japanese sphere of influence by 1914
	Manchu empire, c.1850
	Republic of China, 1914
	Russian empire, c.1850
	Russian territorial gain by 1914
	Russian sphere of influence by 1914
	Russian occupation, 1897–1905
	area allied against *Bakufu*, 1868
	area leased by China to a foreign power
→	Commodore Perry's visits to Japan, 1853 and 1854
→	Japanese campaign, Sino-Japanese war, 1894–95
→	Japanese campaign, Russo-Japanese war, 1904–05
→	Russian campaign, 1904–05
☆	Japanese trading port by 1860
♦	bombardment by western powers, 1863–64
✖	battle, 1894–95
✖	battle, 1904–05
✳	peasant protest or riot, 1780–1850
	Tonghak revolt, 1894
	Japanese industrial area by 1914
——	railroad, c.1914

Japan in the 19th Century

Military bureaucracy (*bakufu*) held sway over Japan from the beginning of the 17th century until the mid-19th century. Under this system, the governor (*shogun*) exercised absolute power and kept close control of the provincial barons (*daimyo*) and the poverty-stricken samurai warrior class. The emperor remained a remote, divine figurehead.

Curriculum Context

Students studying 19th century Japan should focus on changes in its relations with China and the Western powers from the 1850s to the 1890s.

Russian and American ships that attempted to trade with Japan in 1791–92 were repelled. However, after the opening up of California and the 1849 gold rush the United States looked to Pacific countries, including Japan, for new commercial opportunities. The arrival at Uraga in 1853 of U.S. Commodore Perry's "black ships" and his later return in 1854 with warships forced the bakufu's hand; westerners were granted limited trading concessions and Japan's contact with the outside world began.

Repelling invaders

The years following Perry's expedition saw resistance to foreign influence organized by young samurai. Attacks on shipping caused a multinational naval force to bombard the forts at Kagoshima and Shimonoseki in 1863–64. Anti-foreign sentiment grew into concerted opposition to the shogunate. During 1867–68 civil war led to the shogun being replaced by the emperor, in a development known as the Meiji restoration. The emperor moved to Edo (now Tokyo).

Meiji restoration

Period in which Emperor Mutsuhito (known as Meiji the "enlightened ruler") abolished the feudal system and brought in other measures in an attempt to modernize Japan.

Rapid industrialization

Under the new imperial regime, Japan resolved to compete with the west by industrializing, building a modern army and navy, and adopting an aggressive foreign policy, with the intention that Japan should become the dominant power in east Asia. Western expertise was harnessed to build Japan's first light industrial enterprise, a silk-reeling factory. The growth of heavy industry also required the import of western plant and materials—steel, steam engines, and railroad rolling stock were all purchased from overseas.

Expanding the empire

Between 1871 and 1914 Japan achieved dominance in east Asia; the country acquired the Ryukyu Islands, the Bonin Islands (Ogasawara), southern Sakhalin, and the Kuril Islands. In 1894 the Tonghak revolt in Korea reflected a growing socio-economic crisis at home, but this provoked Chinese and Japanese intervention with war erupting between the two powers the same year. Japan defeated China at the Battle of the Yellow Sea and in Manchuria, and took the Pescadores and Taiwan; Korea became briefly independent. Yet intervention by the great powers subsequently deprived Japan of Port Arthur and the Liaodong Peninsula. When Russia was granted a lease on Port Arthur by China and attempted to expand its influence in Korea, Japanese fears grew. Japan negotiated an alliance with Britain in 1902 that effectively neutralized Russia's ally, France, in the event of war, and resolved to confront and overcome its chief rival in the region.

Push into mainland Asia

In 1904 Japanese troops landed in Korea and moved north toward the Yalu. Japanese warships attacked and blockaded the Russian fleet at Port Arthur. On January 1, 1905, the Russian base surrendered. At Mukden Japan defeated the Russian army. Meanwhile the Russian Baltic Fleet arrived in Tsushima Straits too late to relieve Port Arthur. In a historic sea victory, Admiral Togo annihilated the obsolescent Russian fleet. In 1905 by the Treaty of Portsmouth (USA), Russia surrendered south Sakhalin and leases on Port Arthur and the South Manchurian railroad. In 1910 Japan annexed independent Korea. By 1914 Japan had a major sphere of influence in east Asia.

Curriculum Context

The goals and policies of the Meiji state had an important impact on Japan's modernization.

Tonghak revolt

Revolt by a religious movement (Tonghak) against the corrupt and oppressive Korean government.

Britain and India

Throughout the 19th century Britain extended its control across India, making the country "the jewel in the crown" of the powerful British empire.

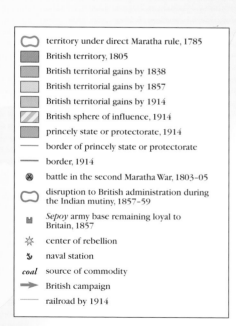

- ⬭ territory under direct Maratha rule, 1785
- ▦ British territory, 1805
- ▦ British territorial gains by 1838
- ▢ British territorial gains by 1857
- ▦ British territorial gains by 1914
- ▨ British sphere of influence, 1914
- ▦ princely state or protectorate, 1914
- — border of princely state or protectorate
- — border, 1914
- ⊗ battle in the second Maratha War, 1803–05
- ⬭ disruption to British administration during the Indian mutiny, 1857–59
- ⋓ *Sepoy* army base remaining loyal to Britain, 1857
- ☼ center of rebellion
- ⤳ naval station
- *coal* source of commodity
- ➡ British campaign
- — railroad by 1914

REPUBLIC OF CHINA
Manchu empire until 1912

Kashgar

Yarkand

Khotan

Kashmir
1846 British protectorate

pindi

Jammu

sugar
Amritsar
Jullundur
Firozpur

acco

Ambala

Saharanpur

Bikaner

Meerut
Delhi *sugar*
Bareilly
Sitapur
barley *wheat* Farrukhabad
Laswari 1804 *barley*
1803 Mainpura
Agra Kanpur
Gwalior Kalpi Fatehpur *sugar*
Allahabad
maize
Jhansi

Jaipur

Ajmer
Nasirabad

wheat

Erinpura

Nimach

Bhopal

HIMALAYAS

NEPAL

TIBET

Lhasa

Sikkim
1817 British
protectorate

Kathmandu
Gurkha War
1814–16

Darjeeling

rice

Bhutan

Northeast
Frontier Agency
1913/14 to Britain

Assam
from 1824 to Britain

Carchar

tea

1868–82 British
protectorate

Manipur

1813 to Burma,
1886 British protectorate

Upper Burma
1886 to Britain

Mandalay

Bundelkhand

rice

wheat

Indore

Mhow

Baroda

Burhanpur

Argaon
1803

Assaye
1803

Amravati *linseed*

DECCAN

cotton

rice *wheat*

tobacco

Poone

cotton

Bijapur

Goa
Goa
Portugal

tobacco

coffee

Mysore
1831 British
protectorate

Bangalore

Seringapatam
1799

Mysore

Tellicherry

Mahé
to France

accadive
Islands

Cochin

Anjengo
Trivandrum

rice

tobacco

cotton
Tuticorin

oil seed

Azamgarh
Benares
(Varanasi)

Danupur

Patna

Baharampur

silk

1857

Lucknow 1857-58

Oudh
1856 to Britain

rice

tea

tobacco

jute

sugar

Dhaka

Bengal

sugar

jute

Chandannagar
to France
Dum-Dum
Calcutta

Chittagong

rice

Tripura

Arakan
1826 to Britain

Burma
Chinese tributary
until 1886

Lower Burma
created 1862 incorporating
Arakan, Pegu and Tenasserim

Pegu
1852 to Britain

Rangoon

Tenasserim
1826 to Britain

wheat

Nagpur

Narmada
Jabalpur

rice

Orissa

Cuttack

Northern Circars

Bastar

Godavari

Aurangabad

Hyderabad

Hyderabad

Krishna

EASTERN GHATS

Yanam
to France

cotton

WESTERN G

rice

cotton

Madras

Madras

cotton

rice
Vellore
Sepoy mutiny, 1806

Pondicherry
to France

groundnuts

Kaveri

Karikal
to France

tea

coconuts

Madurai

Jaffna

rice

Mannar

Trincomalee

Ceylon
1798 to Britain

cotton

Kandy *coconuts*

1815, 1818

Colombo
rice *tea*

Bay of Bengal

Andaman Islands
1857 to Britain

Nicobar Islands
1869 to Britain

1903-04

Gwalior

Ganges

Indus

Jumna

Travancore

Mahanadi

Britain and India

Despite its territorial acquisitions toward the end of the 18th century, the British East India Company still saw its role in the Indian subcontinent as primarily commercial. This was enshrined in the India Act passed by the British parliament in 1784, which forbade further annexation. Nevertheless, British rule (raj) in India continued to grow.

Governor-general

Official appointed by the reigning monarch of a country to act on his or her behalf and govern the realm as the monarch's representative.

One of the reasons British rule spread was that successive governors-general felt obliged to occupy hostile territory or form protectorates to prevent disruption to trade. Thus, when Tipu Sultan of Mysore attacked Travancore in 1789, he saw half his dominions annexed by Lord Cornwallis (governor-general 1786–93) in the ensuing war. Warfare was resumed against the Marathas of central India in 1803.

Expansion of the raj

The fear of an assault on India by Napoleon radically altered British policy. A far more aggressive approach was adopted, in which independent principalities such as Hyderabad were reduced to dependencies by the stationing of British troops there. After the French threat had passed, Company interest turned toward countering Burmese aggression in the east and guarding against Russian incursions from the north. Assam, Arakan, and Tenasserim were acquired from Burma in 1824–26. On the northwest frontier, the First Afghan War (1839–42) was begun against Dost Muhammed; in both this and a later conflict (1878–80), the British occupied Kabul but failed to dominate the country. An attack on Sind secured the Bolan Pass in 1843, while two bloody wars against the Sikhs brought control of the Sikh state of Punjab in 1849. Under Lord Dalhousie (governor-general 1848–56) the empire continued to expand. He evolved the doctrine of "lapse" (when a Hindu prince had no natural heirs his

Curriculum Context

When studying the advance of British power in India up to 1850, consider the efforts of Indians to resist European conquest and achieve cultural renewal.

lands passed to the Company) and, on the pretext of replacing an ineffective government, annexed much of Muslim Oudh in 1856.

Extending British influence

The East India Company also instituted administrative reforms. These began with revision of land revenue collection (the principal source of public finance) and a reorganization of the judicial system along British lines. Despite a Parliamentary directive urging respect for the people's rights and customs, the Company often disregarded religious and cultural sensitivities— particularly under governor-general Lord Bentinck (1828–35), who tried to ban suttee (the immolation of Hindu widows), thuggee (ritual robbery and murder), and infanticide. Continuing Christian conversion, plans to extend roads and railroads, and an insistence on English as the language of education and commerce all threatened the traditional ways of life of both Hindus and Muslims.

Curriculum Context

Important aspects of British rule in India were the changes it introduced to the legal, educational, and other systems central to Indian society and economy.

Members of the British raj (rule) saw themselves as dispensing even-handed justice and the benefits of European civilization to grateful natives.

Challenges to British rule

Opposition to British rule was not, however, anticipated among the Company's sepoy (native) armies. Three such armies had been raised in India; those based at Madras and Bombay were largely untroubled by questions of caste and religion, but the Bengal sepoys—high-caste Hindus and Shi'ite Muslims —were offended by a rumor that new rifle cartridges (which had to be bitten before use) were greased with pork and beef fat. This violated the dietary proscriptions of their religions. Thus began the most serious challenge to British rule in India.

The independence movement

The Indian mutiny (also known as the First War of Independence) began in January 1857 among troops stationed at Meerut and rapidly spread through north central India. The army revolt acted as a catalyst to a number of other grievances, and the mutineers were supported by peasant uprisings and some isolated jihads. The capture of Delhi and the besieging of the cities of Kanpur and Lucknow were serious blows to British authority. However, the Bombay and Madras armies remained largely loyal, and there was no strategy for a national revolt.

Power passes to the Crown

Though brief, the mutiny changed the face of British India; suspicion was now widespread on both sides. The 1858 Government of India Act transferred sovereignty from the East India Company to the British monarch, Queen Victoria, and ended the doctrine of lapse, but other reforms were never instituted. In theory, racial impartiality operated in recruitment to the Indian civil service; in practice few Indians were admitted. The insular community of Anglo-Indians shunned contact with the indigenous population and became ever more prosperous, partly through investment in plantations in southeast Asia and Africa.

Gurkha and Sikh troops from the northwest of India now formed the backbone of the army.

Maintaining frontiers

The British policy in frontier regions continued to be determined by fear of Russian expansion; this led to the Second Afghan War of 1878–80, which ended with the recognition that Afghanistan could not be incorporated within the Indian empire. Similarly, in 1903 the British under Colonel Younghusband invaded Tibet. After a year's conflict, Tibet agreed not to concede territory to a foreign power.

Indian nationalism

Excluded from the administration of their country, educated Indians turned increasingly toward nationalism. The Indian National Congress was founded in 1885 and Gopal Gokhale, its president in 1905, worked for peaceful constitutional progress toward responsible government. The All-India Muslim League, a similarly constitutional organization, was founded in 1906. The Morley–Minto constitutional reforms (1909) brought in a measure of representative government, but Indians were still denied true legislative and financial power.

Indian National Congress

Political party (also known as the Congress party of India) that went onto lead the movement to end British rule in India.

Colonialism and Southeast Asia

By the end of the 19th century European nations and the United States had formed an almost complete colonial network across Southeast Asia.

Calcutta

Chittagong *tea*

Yandabu *tin*

Mandalay

Upper Burma
1886 to Britain

Arakan
1825–52 to Britain

rice

Lower Burma
created 1862

tobacco

Rangoon *rice*
rice

Chiang Mai

Laos
1893 to France

silk

Tongking *tea* Langson
1885 to France ✕1885

Hanoi

Nanning

Zhanjiang

rice Haiphong
1882–83

French Indo-China
founded 1887

Hainan

SIAM *ivory*

rubber Hue

Tourane
(Da Nang)

Annam
1883 to France

1858

1824

Tenasserim
1826 to Britain

tin

rice *tobacco*
Bangkok

Andaman Islands
1857 to Britain

tin *rubber*

Tenasserim

tin

rubber

Cambodia
1863 to France

rice

Mekong

rubber

1859, 1863

Phnom Penh

Plain of
Reeds
Cochin China
1867 to France
rice

Saigon

1859

*Andaman
Sea*

Nicobar Islands
1869 to Britain

tin

rubber

Kutaraja

tobacco
Aceh

Aceh War ✳
1873–1903 *rubber*

rubber

rubber

rubber

tin

rubber

rubber

Sarawak

Sambas

1811

spices

Simeulue

Barus

Nias

rice *ivory*
spices *oil*
Padri War,
1830–39 Indragiri ✳
Tiku *tin*
Padang Sumatra
Painan Jambi
Siberut Batang *ivory* *spices*
Indrapura Miangkabau
Palembang ✳

Bangka

Sukadana

tin

rubber

Belitung

*INDIAN
OCEAN*

Benkulen *spices*
1824 to Netherlands

rubber

Java Se

Bantam

Batavia
(Jakarta)
bauxite Tegal
Java War, 1825–30 ✳
Yogyakarta

Rembang
Japara
Demak
18

Ja

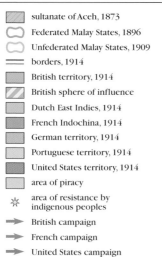

	sultanate of Aceh, 1873
	Federated Malay States, 1896
	Unfederated Malay States, 1909
	borders, 1914
	British territory, 1914
	British sphere of influence
	Dutch East Indies, 1914
	French Indochina, 1914
	German territory, 1914
	Portuguese territory, 1914
	United States territory, 1914
	area of piracy
✳	area of resistance by indigenous peoples
➡	British campaign
➡	French campaign
➡	United States campaign
gold	source of commodity
—	trade route through Malacca Straits

Colonialism and Southeast Asia

Southeast Asia had suffered extensive foreign intervention by the end of the 18th century. While the Dutch seaborne empire in island southeast Asia remained the major European presence, British entrepreneurs had also set up bases for trade with China.

Curriculum Context

Students should consider the influence of natural resources on settlement patterns during French colonial expansion in mainland Southeast Asia.

France's first major expedition into Vietnam occurred in 1858–59, when Napoleon III captured Saigon. The French made further gains, establishing a protectorate over Cambodia and opening Hanoi and Tourane (Da Nang) as treaty ports. In an undeclared war with China (1883–85), France tried to win control of the whole of Indo-China, a goal achieved in 1887 with the merging of Cochin China, Cambodia, Annam, and Tongking as the Indo-Chinese Union (French Indo-China). By 1893 this included Laos. The French urged peasants to sell land to boost rice production; landless peasants then worked in salt and opium factories or for landlords.

The Malay States

During the Napoleonic Wars (when the Netherlands was under French control), Britain attacked Batavia to win control of Java and safeguard its trade routes to China. The administrator Sir Stamford Raffles founded the free port of Singapore in 1819 as a commercial center, stimulating demand for British cotton from southeast Asia and China. In 1824 Britain ceded Benkulen and its claims to Sumatra in exchange for Dutch recognition of British sovereignty over the Straits Settlements. In 1896 the Federated Malay States was set up under a British resident-general. In 1909 other states were acquired from Siam; these formed the Unfederated Malay States. Tin exports increased in the early 1900s and by 1911 nearly half a million hectares of rubber was being grown, mainly on large, European-owned plantations.

Straits Settlements

Province of the East India Company (1826–58) comprising Penang, Port Wellesley, Singapore, and Malacca.

Borneo and Burma

The 1824 treaty had also provided a case for the "White Rajah," James Brooke, to gain British protection for the state he created in Sarawak in 1841. In North Borneo commercial competition for concessions from Brunei and Sulu led to an 1881 royal charter for a British North Borneo Company, which undertook the exploitation of the territory. To protect India's borders, Britain also annexed Burma in the course of three brief wars and administered the country as part of India.

New Guinea

Rival claims to the eastern part of New Guinea saw Germany occupy the northeast and the adjacent islands (renamed the Bismarck Archipelago) and a British protectorate over the southeast of the island. A crown colony in 1888, British New Guinea became a territory of the Australian Commonwealth in 1906.

Driving out the Dutch

After the British withdrew from Sumatra, the Dutch faced opposition from indigenous people in the East Indies. Prince Dipo Negoro's rebellion led to the Java War (1825–29); Tuanku Imam, Minangkabau's leader, fought the Dutch (1830–39); and persistent attacks on merchant shipping by the state of Aceh led the Dutch to declare war in 1873. Thirty years of conflict drained Dutch reserves so that effective occupation of the islands was incomplete by 1914.

Curriculum Context

Students might find it interesting to compare and contrast the differing values, behaviors, and institutions of the Dutch in Indonesia with those of the British in India.

United States of the West Pacific

In 1898, the United States secured the Philippines when Admiral Dewey destroyed a Spanish fleet in Manila Bay. Filipino nationalists, formerly encouraged by the United States to fight for their independence against Spanish rule, felt betrayed and fierce fighting ensued (1902–05). The conflict wrecked the economy and, in addition to military casualties, 100,000 people died from famine.

Latin America

The first half of the 19th century saw the birth of modern independent countries in Latin America.

Legend

- Portuguese colony c.1800
- Spanish colony c.1800
- Republic of Gran Colombia, 1819–30
- united with Mexico 1821–23, independent as United Provinces of Central America 1823–38
- Confederation of Peru & Bolivia 1836–39
- **1838** date of independence as a nation-state
- territory gained by former Spanish colony since independence, with date
- territory gained by the United States from Mexico, with date
- ➡ campaign by Simón Bolívar 1819–24
- ➡ campaign by José de San Martín 1817–22
- ➡ campaign by United States forces, 1846–48
- ⊗ battle fought by José de San Martín
- ⊗ battle fought by Bolívar or de Sucre
- ⊗ battle during the Mexican–American War, 1846–48
- ⊗ battle during the Paraguayan War (War of the Triple Alliance), 1864–70
- ⊗ battle during the War of the Pacific 1879–83
- —— border c.1840
- ---- other border
- —— railroad within Latin America by 1914
- *oil* trade commodity
- ➡ movement of peoples

Latin America

Napoleon's invasion of the Iberian peninsula in 1808–09 was the catalyst for the independence movements in the American colonies of Spain and Portugal. Warfare with France made Spain relax control over its colonies and conflict also caused the Portuguese royal court to move to Brazil.

In the Spanish territories, wars of liberation broke out when Napoleon's brother Joseph Bonaparte took the Spanish throne. Brazil played host to Portugal's prince regent, later João VI, who fled there in 1807 after the French occupied Portugal. When he returned home in 1822, his son Pedro became emperor of an independent Brazil. The new state was recognized by Portugal in 1825.

Mexican unity

Mexico's war of independence, led by the priest Miguel Hidalgo, began in 1810. Hidalgo was executed, but his conservative successor Agustín Iturbide united Mexican society and in 1822–23 formed the Mexican empire with himself as emperor. At the same time, the Spanish colonies in Central America proclaimed a Confederation of the United Provinces, which lasted until 1838, when its constituent parts became individual sovereign states.

Republic of Gran Colombia

Short-lived republic (1819–30) that roughly included the area covered by the modern nations of Colombia, Panama, Venezuela, and Ecuador.

Fighting for freedom

The principal figure of South American independence, Simón Bolívar (the "Liberator"), began his fight to free his native Venezuela and adjoining territories from Spanish rule in 1811. Bolívar's victory at Boyacá in 1819 heralded the proclamation of the Republic of Gran Colombia, and his defeat of the royalists at Carabobo in 1821 led to the fall of Caracas and to Venezuelan independence. In Argentina, revolutionary forces were led by José de San Martín, a veteran of the Peninsular

Simón Bolívar was a remarkable military leader. The country of Bolivia was named in his honor.

War. San Martín trained an army and then led it across the Andes in 1817 to take Lima in 1821. He proclaimed Peru's independence, then gave up control to Bolívar, who established a revolutionary government at Lima. With the final battle of the wars of liberation at Ayacucho in 1824, all Spanish possessions in the Americas became independent, except Cuba and Puerto Rico.

Divided societies

The new states not only inherited the frontiers of the former Spanish and Portuguese administrative regions; social divisions also remained intact. There was no tradition of pluralistic government, and color was still

Curriculum Context

Students should focus on the successes and failures of democracy in Latin America in the decades following independence.

decisive. Spanish-born whites or *peninsulares* (and *reinóis*, the Portuguese equivalent in Brazil) were dominant. The majority of the people (*mestizos* or Indian–Europeans) had limited power while the mulattoes (African–Europeans), *zambos* (Indian–Africans), blacks, and Indians all suffered discrimination. Sectional interests, such as the military, the church, industrialists, bankers, and landlords were often in conflict, and power was frequently seized by *caudillos*, military dictators who ruled through patronage and private armies.

Independence struggles

The caudillo José Francia helped lead Paraguay's struggle for independence and was "el supremo" 1814–40. Bernardo O'Higgins was prominent in Chile's revolution and became supreme director 1817–23. The Mexican Antonio de Santa Anna, after a period as an elected president (1833–36), intermittently took dictatorial powers. During his rule Mexico fought, largely unsuccessfully, against Texas and the United States, and ceded large tracts of land by 1850.

State wars

Intervention by European powers in Latin American affairs was effectively preempted by the Monroe Doctrine of 1823, which signaled U.S. hostility toward any interference in the region from nonregional— effectively European—powers. Most territorial changes

Monroe Doctrine

Policy to prevent European countries from colonizing or interfering with the affairs of the newly independent nations of the Americas; supported by Britain as a means of opening Latin American trade.

The importance of immigrants

Immigrants were among Latin America's greatest assets. Initially they entered Chile and Argentina (which saw a huge influx of Italian immigrants from the 1850s), but Brazil became the preferred destination after slavery was abolished there in 1888. Over one million Europeans arrived in Brazil by 1898; they were favored over the original inhabitants for educational and work opportunities. Chinese and Japanese laborers were also imported in large numbers to work on the railroads and in the mines.

that occurred did so as a result of wars between the new sovereign states. Major conflicts of the period were the War of the Pacific (1879–83), in which Chile defeated Peru and Bolivia, and the War of the Triple Alliance (1864–70), involving Paraguay, Brazil, Argentina, and Uruguay. The 1910–11 Mexican revolution led to chaos, mass slaughter, and eventual U.S. intervention, as U.S. president Wilson supported General Huerta who exterminated the nationalist Zapata rebels while Pancho Villa's bandits ran riot in the north. Wilson sent warships to Tampico and troops to Veracruz in 1914.

Boom and bust

Economic change came swiftly to Latin America. Foreign capital funded railroad and harbor construction; the Panama Canal was completed by U.S. engineers in 1914, after an earlier French venture had failed. British firms exploited the natural phosphates and nitrates of Peru and northern Chile, for use in fertilizers and explosives. U.S. investment turned coffee exports into a vital element in Brazil's economy. In Argentina, revenue from wool, leather, and beef exports brought a sharp rise in the standard of living; meat exports grew after refrigerated sea transport was introduced in the 1880s; but a decline in world trade in the 1890s ended the boom years.

Curriculum Context

The economic transformation of Latin America had important consequences for peasants, immigrant laborers, and others.

The Growth of Canada

Modern Canada was formed when British colonies merged, but it continued to extend its territory as the number of immigrants settling its shores increased.

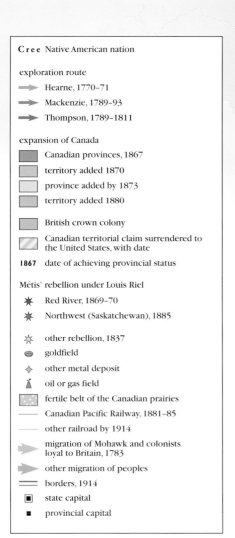

Cree Native American nation

exploration route

→ Hearne, 1770–71

→ Mackenzie, 1789–93

→ Thompson, 1789–1811

expansion of Canada

☐ Canadian provinces, 1867

☐ territory added 1870

☐ province added by 1873

☐ territory added 1880

☐ British crown colony

⬚ Canadian territorial claim surrendered to the United States, with date

1867 date of achieving provincial status

Métis' rebellion under Louis Riel

✳ Red River, 1869–70

✳ Northwest (Saskatchewan), 1885

✵ other rebellion, 1837

⬭ goldfield

✧ other metal deposit

⌐ oil or gas field

▦ fertile belt of the Canadian prairies

── Canadian Pacific Railway, 1881–85

── other railroad by 1914

➤ migration of Mohawk and colonists loyal to Britain, 1783

➤ other migration of peoples

══ borders, 1914

▪ state capital

• provincial capital

Thule

Greenland
to Denmark

Ammassalik

*Baffin
Bay*

Baffin Island

*Foxe
Basin*

Inuit

Inuit

Southampton
Island

Inuit

Inuit

LABRADOR
*1809
to Newfoundland*

NEWFOUNDLAND

erritories
ts 1882–95

Inuit

Inuit

St John's

Newfoundland

*Hudson
Bay*

Churchill

Port Nelson

St Pierre & Miquelon
to France

*James
Bay*

Quebec
(Lower Canada)
1867

Anticosti
Island

Prince Edward Island
1873
*Cape Breton
Island*

*Reindeer
Lake*

Manitoba
1870

Cree

CANADIAN SHIELD

Cree

Europeans

Charlottetown

Abenaki

New
Brunswick
1867

Nova Scotia
1867

Halifax

Cree

*Lake
Winnipeg*

Round Lake

Ontario
(Upper Canada)
1867

Algonquin

Québec

Fredericton

St John

*1842
to US*

*Lake
pigeois*

Ojibwa

*Lake
Nipigon*

Ojibwa

Timmins

cobalt, silver

Cobalt

Papineau's rebellion,
1837

Montréal

Ottawa

extension to
Canadian Pacific
Railroad, 1889

Huron

*Lake
Manitoba*

Winnipeg

Mandan

Fort William

Sudbury

Sault Ste Marie

nickel

Ottawa

*Lake
Ontario*

Mackenzie's protest,
1837

Boston

*Lake
Superior*

Michigan
1783 to United
States

*Lake
Huron*

Toronto
(York)

Rochester

ATLANTIC
OCEAN

Minot

Red River Colony
1818 to United States

Duluth

Fort Erie

Buffalo

New York

Bismarck

Moorhead

Minneapolis

St Paul

*Lake
Michigan*

Detroit

*Lake
Erie*

Cleveland

Philadelphia

City

UNITED STATES

Milwaukee

Pittsburgh

Baltimore

Bermuda
Islands
to Britain

Mississippi

Chicago

Columbus

Washington

Omaha

Des Moines

Indianapolis

Cincinnati

Norfolk

Platte

Missouri

Ohio

The Growth of Canada

The demographic composition of Canada changed markedly with Britain's loss of its 13 American colonies following the American Revolution in the late 18th century. After this conflict loyal colonists, having no wish to be citizens of the new United States, migrated northward.

Curriculum Context

Students are often asked to study causes and consequences of major patterns of long-distance migration. European migrations to America and Canada are good examples to consider.

White loyalists from New York and South Carolina, together with Mohawks who had fought alongside the British, settled in Nova Scotia, New Brunswick, Cape Breton, and Prince Edward Island. Ontario (Upper Canada) saw an influx of new arrivals and the numbers of immigrants from Britain continued to rise. French settlers remaining in Canada after Britain gained control in 1763 (whose rights and customs were enshrined in the 1774 Quebec Act), were overwhelmed. In 1791 the Canada Act provided for a governor and two deputies to oversee the interests of Quebec (Lower Canada) and Ontario. Expansion westward began in 1812, when the Red River Colony (eventually part of Manitoba) was founded by the Earl of Selkirk.

Border disputes

Trouble between British North America and the United States flared up in the War of 1812. A United States invasion of Canada was followed by a British attack on Washington (1814) and the Battle of New Orleans (1815). Thereafter, border issues were settled peacefully: the 1818 agreement on the 49th Parallel created an undefended U.S.–Canadian frontier from the Lake of the Woods to the Rockies, which the 1846 Oregon Treaty then extended to Vancouver.

49th Parallel

Boundary between British and United States territory on the U.S.–Canadian frontier.

Canadian unification

Two rebellions in 1837 resulted in a report that recommended unifying Upper and Lower Canada. Though this was duly carried out in 1840–47, the

American Civil War (1861–65) was the decisive factor in Canadian unification. The Union victory in 1865, attacks by the Fenian Brotherhood on Canadian territory (1866–70), and the westward expansion of the United States caused Canada to press for a union to ensure national security. The British North America Act (1867) united Nova Scotia, New Brunswick, Quebec, and Ontario in the Dominion of Canada. Manitoba joined in 1870, British Columbia in 1871, and Prince Edward Island in 1873. The new government planned to people the Canadian Shield and the Far West, build a transcontinental railroad, and protect farm prices. The Canadian Pacific Railway (completed 1885) played a crucial role in unifying Canada.

Curriculum Context

Students studying Canadian history should focus on the factors that contributed to its nation-building and self-government.

Frontier development

Canada's frontiers continued to expand to the north. In 1912 Manitoba advanced to the 60th Parallel (to match Saskatchewan and Alberta) and Quebec and Ontario were extended to the Hudson Bay and the Arctic. Another frontier developed as Canada's northernmost territories, home to the Inuit, were encroached upon first by fur-trappers and then gold prospectors (notably at the Yukon in the far northwest in 1896). Petroleum companies arrived in Alberta when oil reserves were found there in 1912–14.

Curriculum Context

Canada is often taken as an example of more positive encounters between European migrants and indigenous peoples than the United States. Students could explain how much this reputation is justified.

Indigenous peoples of Canada

The rights and claims of indigenous peoples were largely ignored by the new Canadian state. Many Iroquois, Crees, and Algonquins entered reservations, joined by refugees from the American Indian wars. Some Ojibwa moved into uncharted territories. The Métis of Manitoba (Franco–Indians of mixed-blood) saw their buffalo-hunting culture threatened by immigrants, a process exacerbated by the surrender of the province to the Crown by the Hudson's Bay Company in 1869. The ensuing Red River Rebellion (1869–70) and Northwest Rebellion in Saskatchewan (1885)—both led by Louis Riel—were vain attempts to preserve the traditional way of life of the Métis.

The gradual westward expansion of the United States from its east-coast beginnings was characterized by conflict between white settlers and Native Americans.

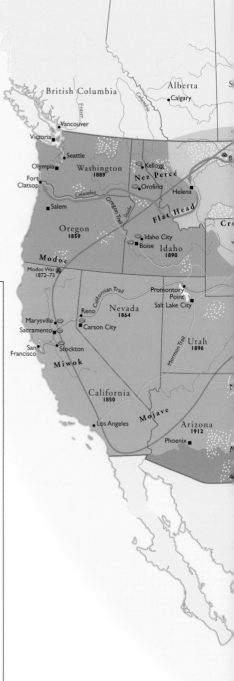

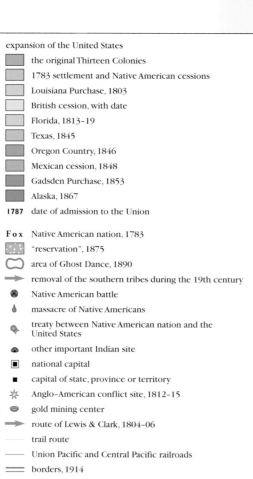

expansion of the United States

- the original Thirteen Colonies
- 1783 settlement and Native American cessions
- Louisiana Purchase, 1803
- British cession, with date
- Florida, 1813–19
- Texas, 1845
- Oregon Country, 1846
- Mexican cession, 1848
- Gadsden Purchase, 1853
- Alaska, 1867

1787 date of admission to the Union

Fox Native American nation, 1783

"reservation", 1875

area of Ghost Dance, 1890

removal of the southern tribes during the 19th century

Native American battle

massacre of Native Americans

treaty between Native American nation and the United States

other important Indian site

national capital

capital of state, province or territory

Anglo-American conflict site, 1812–15

gold mining center

route of Lewis & Clark, 1804–06

trail route

Union Pacific and Central Pacific railroads

borders, 1914

Lake Winnipeg

Lake Winnipegosis

Lake Manitoba

Manitoba

Winnipeg

Red River Colony
1818 to United States

North Dakota
1889

Ft Mandan · Bismarck

Sioux

Standing Rock reservation

South Dakota
1889

Deadwood · Pierre

Wounded Knee
1890

Fort Laramie
1851, 1868

Cheyenne

Denver

Sand Creek
1864

Nebraska
1867

Lincoln · Omaha

Kansas
1861

Topeka · Kansas City

Santa Fé Trail

Medicine Lodge
1867

Oklahoma
1907

Oklahoma City

Kiowa

Red

Canadian

Arkansas

Wichita

Comanche

Colorado

Pecos

Brazos

Texas
1845

Austin

MEXICO
to Spain,
1821 independent

Co

Gulf of Mexico

CANADA
to Britain,
British dominion from 1867

Ontario
(Upper Canada)

Lake Superior

Ojibwa

Minnesota
1858

St Paul

Ottawa

Lake Michigan

Lansing

Michigan
1837

Wisconsin
1848

Fox

Madison

Chicago

Iowa
1846

Des Moines

Tippecanoe
1811

Illinois
1818

Springfield

St Louis

Missouri
1821

Jefferson City

Mississippi

Fallen Timbers
1794

Piankashaw

Indiana
1816

Indianapolis

Greenville
1795

Cumberland Road

Shawnee

Frankfort

Kentucky
1792

Nashville

"Trail of Tears"

Memphis

Tennessee
1796

Little Rock

Arkansas
1836

Chickasaw

Jackson

Mississippi
1817

Louisiana
1812

Choctaw

Mobile

Baton Rouge

New Orleans

Alabama

California & Oregon Trails

Lake Huron

Toronto
(York)

Lake Ontario

Quebec
(Lower Canada)

Québec

Vermont
1791

Montréal

Ottawa

Lake Erie

Ohio
1803

Columbus

US capital from 1800

West Virginia
1863

Charleston

Ohio

Creek

New Echota

Atlanta

Alabama
1819

Montgomery

Maine
1820

Augusta

New Hampshire
1788

Montpelier

Concord

Boston

Albany

Hartford

New York
US capital 1785–90

New York
1788

Pennsylvania
1787

Harrisburg

Trenton

Philadelphia
US capital 1790–1800

New Jersey
1787

Dover

Delaware
1787

Baltimore

Annapolis

Washington

Maryland
1788

Richmond

Virginia
1788

Raleigh

North Carolina
1789

Columbia

South Carolina
1788

Cherokee

Georgia
1788

Jacksonville

Tallahassee

Florida
1845

Seminole

New Brunswick

Fredericton

Nova Scotia

Halifax

1842
to United States

Massachusetts
1788

Providence

Rhode Island
1790

Connecticut
1788

ATLANTIC OCEAN

Nassau

Bahamas
to Britain

Havana

Cuba
to Spain,
1898 independent

The Expansion of the United States

Two decisions made by the Congress of the embryonic United States of America set up the conflict between white settlers and Native Americans. In 1787 indigenous peoples were promised that their lands and property could only be ceded with their consent. Yet four years later, George Washington authorized expansion westward into the Ohio valley.

Initially the growth of the United States was limited by Spain's (from 1800, France's) possession of lands beyond the Mississippi River. However, even at this stage, strong trade links existed between the 13 eastern states of the Union and the Pacific; in time, these would spur westward expansion.

Native American displacement

Expeditions into native territories began in the late 18th century. The Shawnee and Piankashaw succeeded in repelling a group led by General St. Clair in 1791. Yet by 1795, in the Treaty of Greenville, the pattern of substantial territorial gains by the whites and displacement of Native Americans to vacant lands in the west was set. The process was hastened by Thomas Jefferson's purchase of Louisiana from France in 1803, when, at a stroke, the territory of the United States was doubled.

Territorial gains

In the ensuing decades further territories were gained by the United States, either through purchase or conflict: Florida, Texas, Oregon, the Mexican cession, and the Gadsden Purchase. Some 400,000 Native American people were confronted by the westward thrust of settler culture across the Great Plains, enforced by government troops stationed west of the Mississippi River.

Curriculum Context

Some states require that students examine the interactions between Native Americans and European settlers, such as agriculture, trade, cultural exchanges, and military alliances and conflicts.

Gadsden Purchase

Mexican land purchased in 1854. Named for American railway entrepreneur James Gadsden, it comprises a narrow strip of modern southern New Mexico and almost the southern quarter of Arizona.

The Trail of Tears

In Florida, the Seminole people conducted a sustained resistance that was only ultimately suppressed in the 1840s. The forcible removal of the Cherokee to the unsettled "Indian Territory" of Oklahoma in 1838–39, after gold was found in their original homelands, cost 4,000 lives (the "Trail of Tears"). The Delaware, Wichita, and many others suffered a similar fate.

Curriculum Context

In some states students are required to consider how state and federal policies influenced various Native American peoples. The Trail of Tears is a particularly dramatic example to focus on.

Gold prospectors moved onto land that was confiscated from the Cherokee after white settlers found deposits of the valuable metal there.

Staking claims

Settlers annexed Native American lands with the support of the U.S. government: a succession of bills enacted by Congress offering free land in return for minimal investment encouraged claims to be staked to territories on the Great Plains. The encroachment of the railroads further threatened the Plains peoples' main food source, the vast buffalo herds. The once-vast herds had already been depleted by indiscriminate hunting and now became food for railroad workers and the new settlers the trains carried west. Atrocities against Native Americans peaked when the families of Arapaho and Cheyenne who had assembled to sign a treaty at Sand Creek in Colorado in 1864 were slaughtered by a U.S. cavalry contingent.

Reservations

The Federal government tried to end the killing with an Indian peace commission. The Kiowa, Comanche, and Arapaho reluctantly accepted reservation status at the Medicine Lodge Creek Conference (1867), while Sitting Bull's Dakota Sioux ceased hostilities in return for permanent occupation of the Black Hills reservation.

Resistance campaigns

Incursion by gold prospectors into the Black Hills in 1874 provoked resistance by the Sioux aided by the Northern Cheyenne in 1876–77. They annihilated General Custer and 200 of his troopers at the Battle of the Little Bighorn, but their leaders Sitting Bull and Crazy Horse could not capitalize on this victory and they were eventually forced to surrender. The Blackfoot and Crow in Wyoming and Montana, the Modoc in Oregon, and the Nez Percé in Idaho met similar fates. Cochise and Geronimo of the Chiricahua Apaches in Arizona and New Mexico conducted guerrilla campaigns until they were forced to surrender (1872 and 1886 respectively).

Ghost dances

Geronimo's surrender marked the end of the Indian Wars. For the first time in over a century the United States was at peace. However, despair at their situation led many Native Americans to follow Wovoka, a Paiute religious leader. Wovoka conducted ghost dances which, he claimed, would make his disciples immune to gunfire, and he promised that Sitting Bull would

Curriculum Context

Students should understand how displacement of native peoples from their homelands to reservations was a major factor causing resistance to settlement.

Indian Wars

Series of major conflicts between Native Americans and European settlers or U.S. Federal forces, from 1622–1890.

expel the whites. Sitting Bull was murdered while in custody and the U.S. Seventh Cavalry massacred Sioux ghost dancers and their families at Wounded Knee Creek in December 1890.

Industries and plantations

Throughout this period the United States thrived. The northeast saw a stream of immigration from Europe, and new industries arose to feed, house, and clothe the growing population. In the south, the high export prices of cotton brought the development of large plantations. The invention of the cotton gin in 1792 to separate cotton fiber from seeds stimulated production.

Divisions over slavery

Yet the plantation system relied on slavery, a growing point of contention between North and South. In the 1820s, many had hoped to liberate the plantation slaves, but three decades later the rising value of slaves made this less attractive. A compromise was reached when California was allowed to join the Union as a "free" state in 1850 in return for harsh laws against fugitive slaves, but the issue soon exploded into civil war.

Curriculum Context

Analyze how new machines, fertilizers, transport systems, commercialization, and other developments affected agricultural production in various parts of the world.

Curriculum Context

It might be useful to compare contract labor migration and other forms of coerced labor with slavery as methods of organizing commercial agriculture in the Americas in the later 19th century.

The American Civil War

The American Civil War
lasted for four years; the
"War between Brothers"
divided the nation and
caused the deaths of
hundreds of thousands
of people.

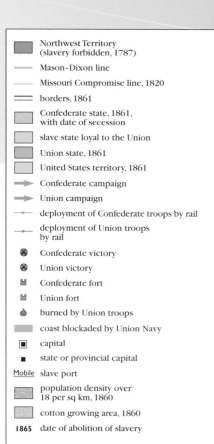

Northwest Territory
(slavery forbidden, 1787)

Mason–Dixon line

Missouri Compromise line, 1820

borders, 1861

Confederate state, 1861,
with date of secession

slave state loyal to the Union

Union state, 1861

United States territory, 1861

Confederate campaign

Union campaign

deployment of Confederate troops by rail

deployment of Union troops
by rail

Confederate victory

Union victory

Confederate fort

Union fort

burned by Union troops

coast blockaded by Union Navy

capital

state or provincial capital

Mobile slave port

population density over
18 per sq km, 1860

cotton growing area, 1860

1865 date of abolition of slavery

Lake Superior

to Michigan

Canada
to Britain

Ottawa

Montréal

Maine
1780

Augusta

New Hampshire
1783

Montpelier

Lake
Huron

Lake
Michigan

Michigan
1836

Lansing

Detroit

Toronto

Lake
Ontario

Rochester

Buffalo

Lake Erie

Cleveland

Ohio
1802

Columbus

Vermont
1793

New York
1799

Albany

Massachusetts
1780

Hartford
Connecticut
1784

Concord

Boston

Providence

Rhode Island
1784

New
York

Long Island

onsin
48

Madison

Milwaukee

Chicago

Illinois
1818

Springfield

Indiana
1816

Indianapolis

Pittsburgh

Pennsylvania
1780

Harrisburg

Philadelphia

Trenton

New
Jersey
1804

ATLANTIC
OCEAN

ria

t Louis

Cincinnati
Newport

Louisville

Frankfort

Perryville
1862

Kentucky
officially neutral though limited support of both sides 1865

Charleston

Virginia
seceded Apr 1861
1865

Mason–Dixon line

Northwestern
counties of Virginia
became the state of
West Virginia in 1863

Harpers Ferry

Gettysburg
1863

Antietam
1862

Baltimore

Bull Run
1861, 1862

Wilderness
1864

Chancellorsville
1863

Richmond

Spotsylvania
1864

Petersburg
1864

Appomattox
Confederate surrender,
9 Apr 1865

Washington

Maryland
1864

Annapolis

Dover

Delaware
1865

Fredericksburg
1862

Cold Harbor
1862, 1864

Hampton
Roads
1862

Fort Monroe

Norfolk

Cairo

Paducah

Bowling
Green

1865

Greensboro

Raleigh

Bentonville
1865

Goldsboro

Fort
Hatteras

Fort Henry
Fort Donelson

Nashville

Tennessee
seceded June 1861
1865

Fort Pillow

Shiloh
1862

Corinth
1862

issippi
d Jan 1861
1865

Meridian
ckson

Stone's River
1862–63
Murfreesboro
1863

Chattanooga
1863

Cleveland

Chickamauga
1863

North Carolina
seceded May 1861
1865

Fayetteville

South
Carolina
seceded Dec 1860
1865

Columbia

Wilmington

Fort Fisher

Fort Macon

Birmingham

Alabama
seceded Jan 1861
1865

Montgomery

Atlanta
1864

Georgia
seceded Jan 1861
1865

Savannah

Charleston

Fort Sumter
Confederate attack
12–13 Apr 1861,
initiates the Civil War

Fort Pulaski

Mobile

Mobile Bay
1864

Pensacola
Fort Pickens

Fort Morgan

Fort St Philip

on

Tallahassee

Jacksonville

Florida
seceded Jan 1861
1865

Gulf of
Mexico

Tampa

Fort Myers

Miami

The American Civil War

The growing demand for cotton as an export crop made the economy of the states south of the Mason–Dixon line (the border between Pennsylvania and Maryland, established 1763–67) dependent on the systematic exploitation of African slaves. On vast plantations, over four million people were denied their rights to family, education, and citizenship.

In deference to southern interests, the Constitutional Convention of 1787 did not expressly prohibit slavery but instead provided for its abolition within 20 years. Yet total proscription was constantly deferred; in the Missouri compromise of 1820, which admitted Maine as a free state and Missouri as a slave state and proclaimed all states above latitude 36° 30′ as free, a convention of balancing abolitionist and slave-owning interests was established. Then a reactionary U.S. Supreme Court ruling of 1857—the "Dred Scott" case—declared that any slave remained a slave forever, destroying the artificial balance between free and slave states and threatening the democratic foundation of the Union. In the 1860 presidential elections all the free states returned the Republican candidate, Abraham Lincoln, who refused to extend slavery to new territories.

Union divided

On December 20, 1860, South Carolina seceded from the Union. Georgia, Alabama, Texas, Florida, Mississippi, and Louisiana soon followed, creating a Confederacy and electing Jefferson Davis as their president. On April 12, 1861, Confederate forces began hostilities with a bombardment of Fort Sumter. Lincoln called for 75,000 northern volunteers, prompting Virginia, North Carolina, Tennessee, and Arkansas to join the Confederacy. Yet not all the slave states seceded: Kentucky declared itself neutral; Delaware, Maryland,

and Missouri remained loyal, as did the northwestern counties of Virginia (which became the state of West Virginia in 1863).

North versus South

A quarter of all those who saw combat lost their lives in the civil war that erupted. The Union government attacked the South to prevent secession of an independent Confederate state. The Union had greater resources, yet superior Confederate generalship caused Union armies several early setbacks, notably at the Battles of Bull Run and failure to take the key town of Fredericksburg. In January 1863, Lincoln espoused outright abolition in his Emancipation Proclamation, freeing all slaves in the Confederacy. The Confederate push north into Pennsylvania was thwarted at the battle of Gettysburg in July 1863. At the same time, Union armies, under the command of Ulysses Grant, advanced down the Mississippi, cutting off Arkansas, Louisiana, and Texas from the Confederacy. Grant fought a series of battles against the Confederate commander Robert E. Lee, which left the South with barely 60,000 troops. Richmond fell on April 4, 1865, and Lee surrendered the Confederate army on April 9. Five days later, Lincoln was assassinated.

Emancipation
The setting free of a person or group of people.

The end of slavery

Lincoln had preserved the Union and freed the slaves, thousands of whom had served in Union regiments. Congress passed a sequence of constitutional amendments: the Thirteenth declared slavery illegal; the Fourteenth gave former slaves American citizenship (native Americans had to wait until 1924); the Fifteenth guaranteed their right to vote. Yet the cultural divide between North and South remained, and Congress could not ensure that African–Americans would be able to exercise their civil rights; racial discrimination survived for the next hundred years.

U.S. Population and Economy

Late 19th-century industrialization and economic growth, driven by an expanding immigrant workforce, helped the United States become a world leader by 1914.

British Columbia

Vancouver Island

Alberta

Saskat

Columbia

Seattle
Tacoma
Olympia Washington
Spokane
Coeur d'Alene riots, 1892–99

Gre
Missouri
Monta

Helena

Butte

Columbia
Portland
Salem

Southern Pacific

Oregon

Snake

Idaho

Boise

Wy

Promontory Point

Union Pa

Central Pacific

Salt Lake City

Reno
Virginia City
Carson City

Nevada

Lead

Sacramento
San Francisco Stockton

Utah

Color

Colorado

Sa

California

Atlantic & Pacific

Los Angeles

Arizona

Southern Pacific

Phoenix

San Diego Yuma

Tucson

PACIFIC OCEAN

RUSSIA

Beaufort Sea

Alaska
1867 ceded to United States,
1912 United States territory

Yukon

Nome
St Lawrence Island

CANADA
British dominion

Fairbanks *Tanana*

Yukon

Anchorage

Bering Sea

Juneau

Kodiak Island

Aleutian Islands

Gulf of Alaska

Queen Charlotte Island

0   1200 km
0   800 mi

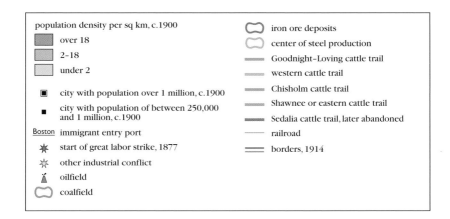

population density per sq km, c.1900

- over 18
- 2–18
- under 2

- ■ city with population over 1 million, c.1900
- ▪ city with population of between 250,000 and 1 million, c.1900

<u>Boston</u> immigrant entry port

- ✹ start of great labor strike, 1877
- ✧ other industrial conflict
- oilfield
- coalfield

- iron ore deposits
- center of steel production
- Goodnight–Loving cattle trail
- western cattle trail
- Chisholm cattle trail
- Shawnee or eastern cattle trail
- Sedalia cattle trail, later abandoned
- railroad
- borders, 1914

N

U.S. Population and Economy

At the end of the Civil War, the northern states experienced unprecedented prosperity as U.S. and foreign speculators rushed to invest in a new wave of industrialization. Railroad construction drove the economy. The completion of the first transcontinental link in 1869 encouraged the development of other lines across the country.

Urban centers and rural areas alike benefited; millions of cattle were transported to slaughterhouses in the new cities of Chicago and Kansas City. By opening up the West to profitable farming, railroads also hastened political change; by 1890 most of the western territories had been admitted as fully-fledged states of the Union. Yet the railroad boom was not without its negative aspects. Corrupt share-dealing provoked a panic and the withdrawal of foreign capital in 1873.

Reconstuction and readmission

The civil war had left the South's principal towns in ruins and its economic life destroyed. Opinion in the North was divided on how to treat the rebel states. President Andrew Johnson (Lincoln's successor) favored reconciliation; hardliners counseled repression. After a period of radical administration, conservatives reasserted white rule in the South, circumventing the constitutional rights guaranteed by Congress to freed blacks. Reconstruction proceeded slowly, and states were gradually readmitted to the Union.

Urbanization and immigration

Towns and cities grew with astonishing rapidity; by 1914, the United States had an urban population of 45 million, most of whom were immigrants. The newcomers were quickly absorbed into the factories of New York, Chicago, Buffalo, Pittsburgh, Cleveland, Milwaukee, Cincinnati, and St. Louis. Appalling

Curriculum Context

Industrialization and immigration are two of the more influential factors that transformed the character of cities in America (and various parts of the world).

conditions prevailed in the crowded cities, polluted factories, primitive mining communities, and harsh lumber camps. Immigrants often faced discrimination; in 1871, Chinese working in mines and on railroads were victims of race riots. Further Chinese immigration was blocked by the Chinese Exclusion Act of 1882.

Strike action

Job losses resulting from the 1873 economic crisis made labor unions hostile to further immigration. The most damaging strike was in 1877: railroad employees, enraged by a pay cut, were supported by a large army of unemployed. Unrest spread to Pittsburgh, Chicago, St. Louis, Kansas City, Galveston, and San Francisco before militiamen suppressed it. This dispute, the first general strike in America, involved millions and spread to Canada. Its most significant feature was deployment of federal troops. In 1892, state militia beat workers at the Carnegie steel mill in Homestead; in 1894 soldiers put down a railroad workers' strike in Chicago.

World leader

The economy, though, stayed buoyant. By 1914, with a population over 97 million, the United States led the world in the manufacture of steel and lumber products, in meat-packing, and precious metal extraction, and had the most telephones, telegraphs, electric lights, and automobiles in the world.

Curriculum Context

Students could compare conditions in cities and in mining and lumber communities in the United States with the social impacts of industrialization in different countries.

Curriculum Context

An important aspect of new inventions, including the telegraph and photography, is the way they transformed patterns of global communication, trade, and state power.

Makers of modern America

The depression in Europe in the late 19th century had little effect on the vibrant U.S. economy, where the rise of magnates made the country the world's great industrial power. John D. Rockefeller dominated the oil industry, Philip D. Armour controlled a meat-packing empire, the financier J. Pierpont Morgan underwrote railroads, and Andrew Carnegie was the leading figure in the steel industry. The symbol of American enterprise was the Model T automobile, first made in 1908 by Detroit mechanic Henry Ford.

Glossary

49th Parallel Boundary between British and United States territory on the U.S.–Canadian frontier.

Afrikaner White inhabitant of South Africa descended from Dutch settlers.

Annexed When one territory is taken over, often forcibly, and incorporated into another territory.

Bastille A prison-fortress in Paris, used primarily for holding political prisoners.

Boxer Uprising Major revolt by Chinese nationalists known as "boxers" that concentrated on attacking the foreign legations in Beijing.

Chartists Group of mainly working class people who supported the "People's Charter," a six-point plan for constitutional reforms.

Clipper Type of very fast sailing ship with multiple masts and square sails, used for carrying freight such as tea.

Concert of Europe Agreement among European monarchies to intervene and crush any rebellions within states, in order to preserve their territorial claims.

Confederacy Government established by southern U.S. states, with its capital in Richmond, Virginia, after seceding from the Union over slavery.

Congress of Vienna International conference from September 1814 to June 1815 to shape Europe after the downfall of Napoleon I.

Crimean War War fought in Crimea, Ukraine, in 1853–56 that arose from British and French mistrust of Russian ambitions in the Balkans.

Dreikaiserbund Alliance of Germany, Austria-Hungary, and Russia. It aimed to neutralize the rivalry between Germany's two neighbors and to isolate Germany's enemy, France.

Emancipation The setting free of a person or group of people.

Enlightenment Movement that rejected traditional ideas and values in favor of reason and individualism, and led to humanitarian reforms.

Entente Cordiale Usually translated as "friendly understanding," the term refers to an agreement between France and Britain to cooperate over colonial interests.

Eureka uprising Rebellion of gold miners against police and military authorities that marked the emergence of Australian democracy.

First Coalition First of the military coalitions that were formed by European powers to invade France in order to prevent the spread of revolutions to their own countries.

Free trade The abolition of import tariffs protecting local producers from competition.

Gadsden Purchase Mexican land purchased in 1854 by the United States.

Governor-general Official appointed by the reigning monarch of a country to govern the realm as the monarch's representative.

Imperialism When a country extends its power by dominating another country and ruling over it.

Indian National Congress Political party (also known as the Congress Party of India) that led the movement to end British rule in India.

Indian Wars Series of major conflicts between Native Americans and European settlers or U.S. Federal forces, from 1622–1890.

Irish famine The failure of the staple potato crop in Ireland, owing to a plant disease; one-third of the population starved to death.

Maronite Christians Large Roman Catholic Christian community of Arabs, centered in Lebanon.

Meiji restoration Period in which Emperor Mutsuhito (known as Meiji, the "enlightened ruler") abolished the feudal system in an attempt to modernize Japan.

Monroe Doctrine Policy to prevent European countries from interfering with the affairs of the newly independent nations of the Americas.

Partition Division of a single country into separate areas with different governments.

Pogrom Organized attack on or massacre of a community of people, usually for religious or ethnic reasons.

Republic of Gran Colombia Short-lived republic (1819–30) that roughly included the area covered by the modern nations of Colombia, Panama, Venezuela, and Ecuador.

Sphere of influence The hinterland of a coast occupied by a European power.

Straits Settlements Province of the East India Company (1826–58) comprising Penang, Port Wellesley, Singapore, and Malacca.

Tonghak revolt Revolt by a religious movement (Tonghak) against the corrupt and oppressive Korean government.

Further Research

BOOKS

Bowman, John S. and Maurice Isserman (Editors). *Exploration in the Age of Empire, 1750–1953* (Discovery and Exploration). Chelsea House Publications, 2009.

Collins, Mary. *The Industrial Revolution* (Cornerstones of Freedom). Children's Press, 2000.

Frader, Laura Levine. *Industrial Revolution* (Pages from History). Oxford University Press, 2008.

Hillstrom, Kevin. *The Industrial Revolution* (American History). Lucent Books, 2008.

Lynch, Michael. *The British Empire* (Teach Yourself). McGraw-Hill, 2005.

Nardo, Don. *The Industrial Revolution in Britain* (Library of Historical Eras). Lucent Books, 2009.

Roberts, J. M. *The European Empires* (The Illustrated History of the World, Volume 8). Oxford University Press, 2002.

Roza, Greg. *America's Transition from Agriculture to Industry: Drawing Inferences and Conclusions* (Critical Thinking in American History). Rosen Central, 2005.

Stalcup, Brenda. *Turning Points in World History—The Industrial Revolution*. Greenhaven Press, 2002.

Stein, R. Conrad. *The Industrial Revolution: Manufacturing a Better America* (The American Saga). Enslow Publishers, 2006.

Stimpson, Bea. *The World of Empire, Industry, and Trade* (Quest History Series, Volume 3). Trans-Atlantic Publications, 2000.

Wilkes, Aaron and James Ball. *Industry, Reform, and Empire*. Folens, 2009.

INTERNET RESOURCES

American History. A Smithsonian Institution site with many relevant themed links including work and industry, technology, and immigration.
http://americanhistory.si.edu/onthemove/themes/

British Empire. A rich resource on British imperialism with illustrations, maps, and links.
www.britishempire.co.uk/

Historyworld.net. A range of web pages and links about the industrial revolution.
www.historyworld.net/wrldhis/PlainTextHistories.asp?historyid=aa37

James Logan High School. This school site has a list of useful links to pages about imperialism in India, Africa, and Asia.
www.jlhs.nhusd.k12.ca.us/Classes/Social_Science/Imperialism/Imperialism.html

Library of Congress. Website with pages linking to various relevant topics such as city life and railroads.
http://memory.loc.gov/learn/features/timeline/riseind/riseof.html

Public Broadcasting Service. A vast selection of websites on different themes, many linked with PBS TV shows, including historical.

Empires: A very useful section focusing on Queen Victoria's reign as figurehead of the vast British Empire.
www.pbs.org/empires/victoria/

History detectives: This section has links to invaluable evidence pages about industrialization in the U.S. 1870–1900.
www.pbs.org/opb/historydetectives/investigations/era_industrialization.html

Small Planet. Teacher resources that are relevant for students too, notably the Age of Imperialism section.
www.smplanet.com/imperialism/toc.html

Whittier College. This site is a copy of a lecture encapsulating the nature and causes of imperialization, including details on advances in firearm technology.
http://web.whittier.edu/academic/history/worldhistory/Imperialism.pdf

Index

Page numbers in *italic* refer to illustrations.